BRAHMA

A Hybrid Graphic Novel

Akhilesh Asokan

You'd hardly expect 'Corporate Tax' and 'Fantasy Thriller' to coexist in a mental space. Further, you'd never fathom a number crunching, jargon juggling Chartered Accountant with an Executive MBA from Harvard to delve into the realms of demons and fiendish creatures. Akhilesh balances the order of his busy analytical day by dreaming up stories after work hours. In contrast with his disciplined corporate life, Akhi spent a vivid childhood playing in the dirt, fishing for tadpoles and chasing after dragonflies to see if they could actually breath fire. The evenings spent in his ancestral home, he effortlessly dispensed to his cousins, tall tales from his school built over a graveyard and stories of his math teacher who he was certain, moonlighted as a vampire. Akhi credits his imagination to folklore narrated by his grandparents, urban legends brewed by simple village folk and the surreal dreams that usually pushed him off his bed at night. Akhi nourished these stories and tales from his childhood, and today, he attempts to bring them out through new age media. His pet project called 'A Small Big World' is an initiative that forages stories from micro-cultures and adapts them through contemporary media like graphic novels, and video games. And between all this, he has also found the time to qualify as a Certified Management Accountant from the Institute of Management Accountants in the United States. Akhi's friends are entirely certain that he hides away in his home, a contraption that enables him to stretch and bend time.

After his eighteen hour shift as Director at a reputed conglomerate in Dubai, Akhi studies politics, conspiracies, espionage, criminology and horror films after which he sleeps with the lights on.

Sujith Sugathan

People have reported to have heard triumphant evil scientist laughs and at times, expletives from Sujith's work area. Growing up, the only things he outgrew were his clothes. His love for comics, fiction and tinkering kept up. An engineer and MBA by education, Sujith bungeed into the creative side after realizing that MBAs were expected to wear ties and pants that didn't include copper rivets in them. Having worked as an art director and advertising professional, Sujith is today an independent creative consultant dabbling in writing, photography, corporate films, sculpting and musical instrument building. On a regular day, Sujith can be found tinkering away in his sawdust filled lair infested with antiques, musical instruments and power tools.

On the literary front, Sujith is fascinated with Classical Science Fiction, Absurd Fantasy, folklore, mythology and graphic novels. Atop his bookshelf, along with the works of Terry Pratchett, Bill Bryson, RK Narayan, Douglas Adams, Garry Larson, Khushwant Singh, Moebius, Will Eisner, Albert Uderzo, and Neil Gaiman rests a sign that reads 'Borrow along with the bullet I put in your head'. Violent, but it apparently works.

BRAHMA

Akhi
&
Sujith (Co-Author)

Kairali Books

English Language
Brahma
(Novel)
by
Akhi & Sujith (Co-Author)

♦

Published in November 2024
by Kairali Books Private Limited
Thalikkavu Road, Kannur.
Ph : 0497-2761200
E-Mail : Kairalibooksknr@gmail.com

♦

Concept
Akhi

♦

Visualization
Sujith

♦

Production & Project
Anu C Raj

♦

Illustrations
Anish T K

♦

98/24-25/Sl.No.1665/250/130 gsm art paper
ISBN 978-93-5973-138-4

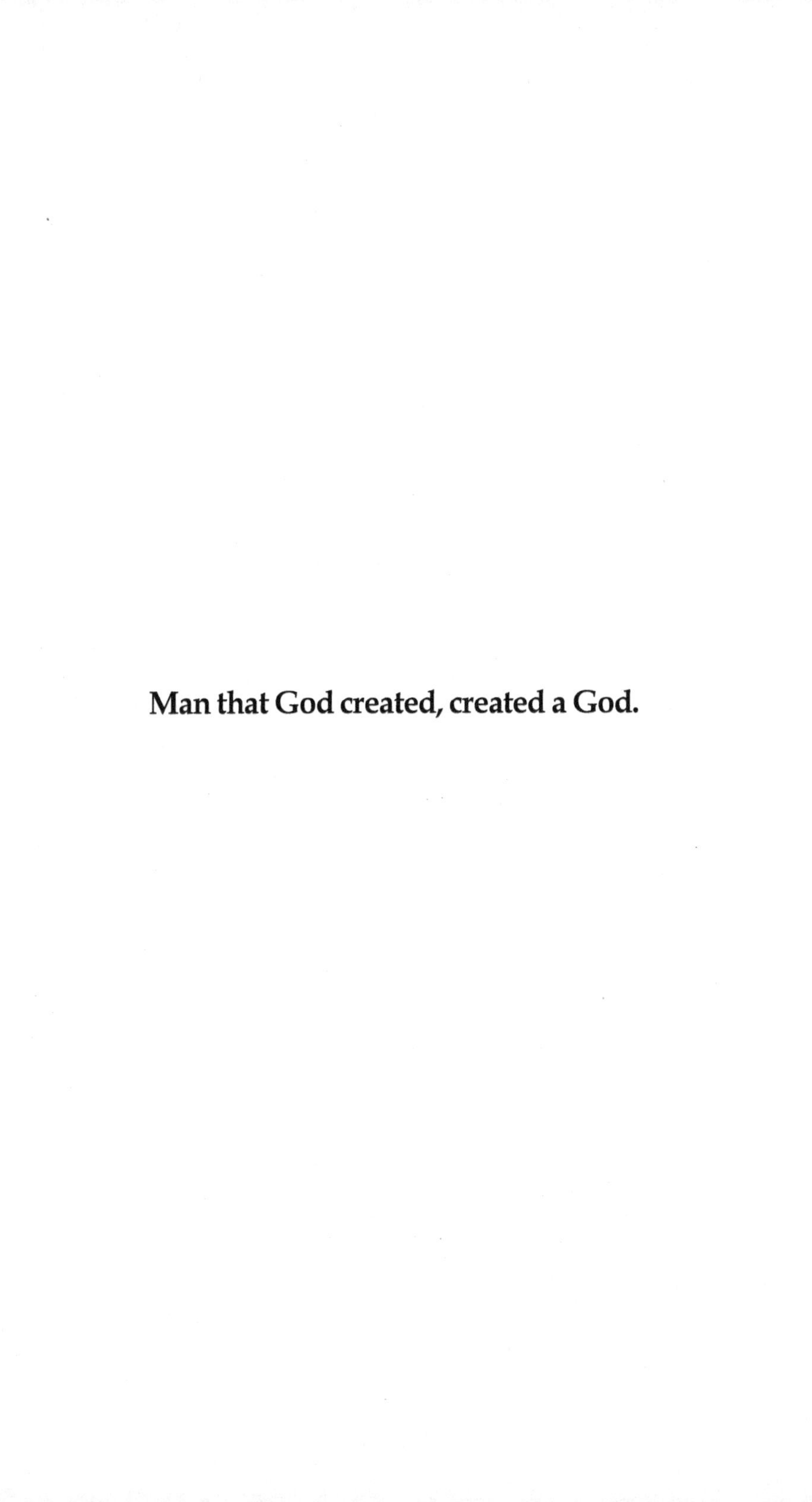

Man that God created, created a God.

Chapter 1
Oberalp

Castle Oberalp, 1804 AD

Are prayers ever answered?

Is there a lord in heaven who answers prayers?

Running, gasping, Amelia prayed. Not knowing if they would be answered. Not knowing if she would make it through that night.

Amelia ran mindless. Amelia prayed with all heart. She didn't know what she ran from. She didn't know what she had seen. She cursed the questions that flooded her mind and prodded her to investigate that which was forbidden. Amelia prayed as she ran with all her life. Life, Amelia didn't know how much of it was left.

The horrors she stood witness to at the Northern chamber, She had brought that upon herself. She could have chosen not to tread there like Charles had warned. But the Charles that returned from India was not the man who had left Oberalp a year ago. India had done something to Charles. Amelia wanted to turn back time. But all she could do was run.

The walls behind her turned black. Amelia looked over her shoulder. She didn't want to. But she had to. A storm of red dust followed her in a maddening haste. And from the dust snarled grotesque faces. Faces formed out of red dust. Coagulating and breaking apart at will from form to form. Letters covered the walls as the red storm devoured space.

The storm grew more furious and its demons louder. Amelia ran. Amelia prayed harder.

David would lose his mother tonight. All Amelia wanted was to see him one last time. The search for David's nanny had brought this upon her. Amelia didn't have to quench the questions that filled her mind after her servants went missing one after another. She knew the Northern Chamber held the answers. Now, she regretted that it did. Amelia ran.

In the midst of the red dust and the turbulence of demonic faces, sat poised, watching… him… it. The corridors of Oberalp seemed longer than they had ever been. Amelia stumbled. The demons of red dust tried to reach out and grab her. Amelia prayed. Amelia cried.

That cursed night she hunted for answers. The night she watched from a gap in the door, an ungodly creature that shared her walls. That night would be her last. The answer now, hunted her.

Amelia ran for one of the rooms. Her body struck on the door that refused to budge, against all expectations. She banged restlessly as the splinters drove into her palms. She ran from door to door crying and shouting. Her screams were silent. The fear of the beast she had seen suppressed every sound from her belly. Amelia tried to run. Her body trembled. She clung to the walls, her feet slipping on hot whale oil that dripped on the floor. She banged one door after another till her legs could no longer run. Fatigue laced with scare had taken over.

She crawled to the last door. The only door to which her feet could carry her. She no longer had the might to bang. Her palm fell lifelessly on the wood. Her last futile attempt to convene attention. The red storm behind her gained footing moving faster. Howling and screeching. Covering the walls of the hallway with horrendous figures. Figures that refused to stay still. Amelia screamed silent through her lungs dry of blood.

A loud thud followed the dissonance of wood abrading against stone. The door swung open.

'Brahmaaaa'

The voice from the bowels of the room filled the hallway. Breaking through the howls of the creatures in the storm. Fracturing their purpose to reach for the prey. Stillness followed the voice as it echoed on rattling stone walls.

The voice did something. Through the strands of hair that covered her face, Amelia saw the darkness pull itself back to the propagator. The demons retracted to the master. At the end of the passage, he…it watched in cold silence as Charles stood at the door. Amelia felt her face depart the cold floor. Warm hands held her close. 'Charles'. Amelia wanted to say. She looked up at his face as her eyes shut. She didn't need to run anymore.

Castle Oberalp, a stronghold of the French Command. A fortress that kept away everything external. And now a fortress that contained everything within it. Everything.

The morning breeze ran through the land taking its time through the trees and leaves. Through an open window, the breeze made its way and ran along Amelia's hair. For a moment, she snuggled. And then like water breaking through rammed earth, came crashing the thoughts from the night

before. Amelia sprang up from her bed. She looked around gasping for breath. She ran to David. The baby slept peacefully.

Amelia rushed out of the room. The servants went about their daily business puzzled. It was not every day they saw the Lady in an unkept form. Charles was in a meeting with his lieutenants. He looked up from the desk and saw Amelia trembling by his door. He excused himself and stood up. 'Love, perhaps this morning springs more surprises on me than I would have wanted. What haste brings you to my chamber in this rather ungainly attire? I always welcome your reforms, you know that. But some, I'm rather forced to lovingly refuse. The Lady of the house walking around in her night clothes is one of them. Go on and deck yourself in threads that honor your beauty' Charles smiled and gently led her back to the room. Amelia had nothing to say. All she could do was keep looking at him. Charles spoke like he bore no memory from the previous night. Not a speckle of fear.

Maybe, it was all, just a dream. Everything she thought she saw at the Northern tower, the red storm down the hallways of Oberalp. Everything felt like a dream now. Amelia prayed that it was. She wasn't sure. How could dreams feel ever so real or reality feel like a dream? As she stood watching the light creep through the morning country outside the castle, her mind brimmed with questions of the plots within.

Curiosity can be stronger than fear. And for Amelia who was headed to the Northern Tower, curiosity would give her the answers for everything that was happening around her. A part of her heart kept questioning her intent. It kept reminding her of her dream the previous night. Curiosity silenced the questions. She had to do this to prove her sanity. If not to anyone else, to herself. Curiosity shadowed fear.

That night, Amelia inched through the darkness. The sound of her heart pounded on her ears. But she had to know. The large door of the main chamber of the tower stood before her. Red light streamed out through the gap between the doors. The gap invited Amelia to look through it. Fear stood aside and the desire for answers had come forth. Amelia held her breath and looked through.

In the middle of the stone-walled room sat a creature with one leg touching the ground and the other folded in. A creature held reminiscence of its once human form. Long golden fangs shot out from his mouth. And from his fingers, long golden claws. Lone strands of hair ran down his neck. His flesh looked burnt and from between the scars were incantations in red. The creature from her dream.

Lying lifeless on his lap was a figure that Amelia had seen before. She knew the man. She stretched her neck further into the room. The red light fell on a face that Amelia recognized in shock. It was Charles.

Amelia wanted to scream. Fear and shock silenced her. The creature lifted his left arm with the grace of a dancer. He spread his fingers along with the long golden claws that were driven into them.

'*Aham Jighasmu*' shouted the creature driving his claws into the waiting body on his lap. With both hands, the creature shredded Charles. Blood splashed all over the room. Demons from the red dust began to bathe in the blood. Amelia's white face fell upon Charles's eyes.

'Run' He said without a voice. Amelia broke out of her trance. She had to get to her baby.

She turned around to run back, but the stairway that brought her to the room had disappeared. An entire stairway! Amelia looked around. Before her, emptiness stood questioning her memory. She bolted the room behind her in a desperate attempt to contain the creature within it. The creature that had killed her husband. Amelia tried to climb down the landing of the staircase. She didn't know what else to do. There was not much she could do.

Heavy hands banged against the door. Amelia hung down by her arms. The door above her shattered and red light filled the darkness. Amelia let go. She fell. This was definitely not a dream. Amelia could feel her fingers ache. Amelia would not see Baby David again. This fall would see the end of her. Her questions, unanswered, she would die. Amelia prepared her mind for the pain that awaited her. Amelia prepared her body to bleed to death on the cold ground of Fort Oberalp.

The ground seemed softer than Amelia could have imagined. It splashed all over and around her. Amelia had drowned in the ground. The ground entered her ears and nose, suffocating her. The ground had turned into water. Amelia stood up. Drenched but not dead.

She stood in a courtyard filled with water to her knees. And this was not a courtyard in Obcralp. On all four sides of the courtyard were raised verandas with wooden pillars. Wooden pillars with carvings of elephants and lions. Pillars that Amelia had never seen before. And above the verandahs, stood another floor. And, more pillars. She heard the laughter of a child and another of a woman who seemed to be calling out for the child. She could not see anyone. Just voices and soon the voices died too.

Amelia kept turning around frantically trying to find rationality in the new environment.

From the long passageway by the verandas, Amelia heard a loud roar. And by every passing second, the roar got louder. Amela didn't want to know the creature behind the roar. She climbed out of the water onto the veranda and ran through a passage in front of her. Not that she knew where she was going, but that was the only way that seemed to take her away from the roar that followed.

At the end of her path, she saw familiar stone walls. Walls of Oberalp. As Amelia ran, she heard loud footsteps behind her. She looked back. Again, with fear-filled curiosity. Fear, more than curiosity.

Amelia was being chased by a thin bald man draped in red. Inscriptions marked into his skin all over the body. He held a large wooden altar of sorts made of dark wood. Infernal creatures carved into the structure held their clawed hands out of the frame reaching out for the prey their carrier chased.

'Baishkaaa'

The roar of the pursuer filled the darkness around Amelia. From a distance, she recognized David's room. Amelia rushed through the door and bolted it shut. She ran to David and grabbed him from the crib. Amelia looked around the room. She saw a large wooden chest. Climbing in, she shut the lid.

It was only now that she looked at David's face. David slept peacefully. Oblivious of the fact that his father had died in the hands of an impious creature. Oblivious of the fact that the fiendish lot from hell had been chasing his mother. 'Lord in heaven, save me from this darkness.' Amelia prayed in silence. Silencing her cries to save her child from the creature that chased her.

Oberalp stood facing the morning sun. The stone walls of the fort were built to take all attacks from invasions. A driveway standing on large columns stretched out to the fort from a nearby hill. A river that sprang from the hills flowed under the driveway. The view of the country around Oberalp could fuel a poet. But the view was deceptive.

The creature she saw in the Northern Chamber; The demon that left her child without a father; The godless being she ran from sat beside her studying her child. David was attracted to the shining gold in his claws. He reached out for it.

Amelia woke up and looked to where she saw the creature. There was no one. David slept. Amelia climbed out of the chest taking care not to wake up her baby. The morning light made its way through the window. Amelia had to get out of Oberalp. Demons fear daylight, she thought.

Amelia ran out of the room into the empty corridor. The torches on the wall had all burnt out and she could smell the oil in them from the previous night. Amelia ran without looking back till she came to the opening into the front yard. And then, she stopped. Shocked and puzzled.

Charles Dieudonne Aubert, Second Grade Commandant of the French Army was mounted on his horse galloping out of Oberalp. The same man who Ameilia watched die.

Amelia's lips went dry. She tried to call out to Charles. She couldn't. She questioned her sanity. All in silence.

'You missed him again'.

A voice in a foreign accent.

Amelia turned around to look at the foreigner. His face glowed. He stood calm with pride. She did not like him.

'You are the priest who came from India with Charles.' '*Thirumeni* to you, Madame Aubert.'

Amelia was still lost. But in her present mental state, she said to herself 'Savage', before she turned around and left.

Amelia spent the rest of the day recounting what had happened. She had watched Charles die and rise again. And all that was not a dream. Sorcery and witchcraft were the only things she could blame everything on. Eastern sorcery and witchcraft. But Charles, had he taken the path to hell?

Amelia had to confront Charles that evening. She wanted an explanation for everything. The door to his chamber was half open. As she walked in Amelia saw the sight that proved her fears. Charles stood bare-chested facing away from her. He stood cold, without expression applying ashes on his body from an urn that bore the incantations she had seen the previous night. Amelia's knees gave way. She kneeled on the ground crying.

'Lord in Heaven, The Devil is upon you! How could you take to black magic? What is it that you don't have?'

Amelia wanted answers.

Charles tried to hold her. She moved away. 'You do not comprehend the curse that is upon us. What I have brought upon this house. But learn this, I do this for us. And there is no other way. I have no other choice, Amelia. I don't expect you to understand. You cannot understand. All I ask of you is to leave Oberalp tonight. Take our son far from here and never come back.'

And saying that, he stood up determined. Amelia tried to reason with Charles. She cried. Cried out loud. Charles pushed Amelia out of his chamber. She tried to talk to him. To understand what was happening.

Amelia struck the locked door. Again and again. She banged hard. She cried. And finally, the door opened. Amelia ran into the chamber to try and convince Charles. But the chamber was no more the same as it was moments ago. The chamber, full of Charles's books and table, was empty now. The walls and floor, all empty, stretched across.

From a distance, Amelia heard the cry of a child. She ran towards the voice. On the floor of the room, was now a deep well. The cry came from the well. Amelia kneeled to look down the well and at the bottom she saw her child strung to a bed made of red rope. Amelia climbed down the well and freed her baby. She looked around and saw no one. As she clambered up the walls of the well, came a voice.

>*'The blood that runs the master's flesh, will hold the reins in moons to come. I will bestow upon him then, the rights to the Yoktra'.*

Amelia ran out of Castle Oberalp with her crying baby in hand. Promising never to return to know the truth. Praying that the truth, would stay within the walls of the castle.

Chapter 2

Lure

November 12, 2023, Schwarzenberg

'The haunted have turned haunters on this land. The gruesome deaths they died, give them the right. Don't you think so?'

Aubry sat watching the bubbling spring water as it cooked the rye bread in the iron pot.

'What do you expect out of unholy land such as this? The ground stinks of the rotting flesh of Pontius Pilate. The man took The Lord to the cross. They say his body floated all the way here after he killed himself. Pontius rises every Good Friday, they say. To wash his hands in the waters of Lake Pilatus. Wash his hands off the blood!'

'Easy there, Cousin Aubry. You're frightening Shorty here'. Mark didn't look up from his cup of hot coffee. It was cold as hell, he wanted the coffee badly. Shorty sat on a rock rubbing his hands. He looked for something to throw at Mark.

'Yeah Shorty, is the man scaring you with his boo boo stories Shorty?'

Jules ran her hand on Shorty's snowcap.

'Die in hell Jules'. Shorty untied Jules's boots.

'Come on Aubry, aren't these cockamamie stories you locals cook up to scare the tourist?'

Paul had sat through the entire story waiting to pick on Aubry at the end. He bit into a piece of hot rye bread.

'Much like the bread you cook in the hot springs.'

'Nothing like the bread Paul. These are strange grounds. There are things we are meant to understand and others we shouldn't try at all.'

Aubry's face ran pale and his voice deep. Shorty was getting a little uncomfortable.

'Shouldn't we get going?' Shorty erupted before Aubry went into details that would keep him up at night.

'Mark, say hi to Gran for me. Stick to the map and you should be home before supper. And remember, you take a right after the railway station'.

Aubry packed the rest of the rye bread for the trip. Shorty pushed everyone into the car. He, in particular, wanted to be off the road before night.

'I left this place when I was 10, need a map to find my way around here' Mark got on the wheel and propped up his phone.

'The stories the locals make up! The Ghost of Pontius something.

Jules leaned back and put her feet on the dashboard. 'Feet off Jules!'

'You never know Jules, these things could be true' Shorty

wiped the mist off the glass onto his side. The car ran by a lake. The water was black with the exception of a few blocks of ice. Shorty looked carefully at something floating on the water. A bloated body of a man tossed around hitting the ice. Shorty screamed and Mark slammed the brakes. Mark pulled off his seatbelt, kneeled on his seat and cupped Shorty's face.

'What the hell Shorty!'.

'A man… in the lake…floating…there' Shorty shivered. 'There is nothing there'.

Jules got out of the car. Paul still recovering from the shock, looked out through the window and whacked Shorty on the head.

'I did see something'.

'Something? You probably saw a fish or SOMETHING'. Jules got back into the car.

'Or was it the Loch Ness monster, baby brother?' Jules reached out and pitched Short's cheeks.

'Damn Aubry, scared the daylights of this imbecile. Now we have to deal with him through the trip.' Mark stepped on the pedal.

The rest of the journey was peaceful. Shorty had put himself to sleep. The other three were not pleased. The midday sleep would give Shorty the excuse to stay up all night and demand company. Shorty did that when they watched horror movies. He pretended to want to play board games through the night just to keep everyone in his room.

Mark followed the map. White mountains were all they could see, an occasional cabin breaking the visual monotony. The road was straight and empty until Mark saw an obstacle which by the second, grew in size. He slammed the brake hard propelling Paul and Shorty out of their seats. Jules was woken up. She cursed louder than the brakes. 'Now what?'

'Where the hell did he come from?' Mark looked furiously. 'Hey looser, get off the road.'

Jules unbuckled her seatbelt preparing to get out. She was in the mood for a fight.

'No road through here'. The man stood unshaken by the loud interruption behind him. He warmed his hands on a fire.

'Are you kidding me, get off the road'. Mark unbuckled his seatbelt.

'You should check the map my friend. There is no road through here'.

Mark pinched the map on his phone. The man was right. He had hit a dead end. But then, the road was there a minute ago. 'Get back into the car and drive Mark' Jules was losing her patience.

'Now who is seeing stuff?' Shorty was happy he had company. Someone to pick on for the rest of the trip. Mostly to keep attention off himself.

'The map said to steer left and now, there is no road.'

'Yeah, Mark, the Google lady is messing with you. Creepy old bugger that.' Shorty was enjoying it when he could.

'First Shorty loses his bearings, then Mark almost kills a homeless man. How much did you guys drink last night?' 'Shut up! Jules'

'Yeah, shut up Jules'. Shorty was quick to add on.

'Jules, will you put Aubry on the speaker? I need to check the route with him.'

Aubry answered in a couple of rings.

'Man! Think I messed up. We were following the map and took right after the railway station. But that was a dead end. Hey, it's starting to fog up. Can you see ahead Jules?' Mark slowly stopped the car.

'Can't seem to see a thing'.

The fog filled the entire landscape around them. It got colder. 'What's that?' said Shorty pointing.

The windscreen was filled with writing. As they watched, letters appeared all over. Thousands of small alphabets from a language none of them had seen before. Too many for anyone to have just written them.

'It's everywhere!' 'Writings'

'What's everywhere, Mark, Jules, Paul, Shorty…what do you see?' Aubry was still on the phone.

'They are everywhere!' 'What is everywhere?' "Get out of the car'.

Mark tried to unbuckle his belt. It had never been this difficult to unbuckle a seatbelt, but when one's hands are trembling, it could be. They jumped out of the car and moved away.

'Guys where's Shorty?'

Mark looked around. Saw nothing.

Jules and Paul slowly walked forward through the snow trying to keep each other in site. The fog grew thicker and they walked back shouting out to Shorty. Trying to stay together. A hand shot through the fog and held Paul by the neck.

'The blood of the innocent will kill the man within'. Shorty exited through the fog strangling Paul. The fingers drove into his skin. The inscriptions they had seen on the windscreen were now on Shorty covering every inch of his skin. His eyes looked lifeless.

'Cut it out Shorty!'.

Paul and Jules ran to Shorty. By then he had Paul on his knees. Paul was struggling to get loose. Mark caught Shory by the shoulder and pulled him back. Jules joined him to find Shorty stronger than she had ever seen him. They had wrestled in the past. But Jules had always managed to get him to cede. Not this time.

Shorty slowed down. 'Why are you two holding me'. Shorty asked puzzled. The letters had disappeared from his body. Mark and Jules let go of him. 'What's going on guys, why were you holding me?'

Jules and Mark were more confused than Shorty was.

'Will kill…the man within'.

They heard a voice from behind them.

Paul, now had the marking all over him. He stood up and grabbed onto a log nearby. Furiously, he hurled it towards Mark hitting him on the neck. He swung again. This time at Shorty. Shorty fell to the ground, bleeding from the knee down.

'The blood of the innocent will kill the man within'.

Paul raised the log above his head and prepared to swing it on Shorty on the ground. Shorty, bleeding and helpless, cried.

Jules pulled herself up and ran over to Paul knocking him down with her shoulders. Her brutish momentum knocked Paul off his feet. Both of them landed on the ground with bone-splitting force. Paul stood up and looked over to Mark and Shorty, both bleeding all over. 'What's happening here Mark, Shorty?'. All three men were clueless.

'You were going to kill me' shouted Shorty. They looked around for Jules. A few feet away from where the men fell, they saw an outline in the fog. They strained their eyes and moved closer. 'Jules, is that you?' As they got closer, they saw Jules sitting on the ground whispering to herself. 'Jules' Shorty called out. Jules looked up and pulled up the log from behind her. And then, started to lick the blood that covered it.

'The blood of the innocent, will kill the man within.'

She whispered at first and then started shouting. But Jules sat there without trying to get up. The fog got thicker and faded. And with it, took Jules. Shorty, Mark and Paul looked around without saying a word. They were too shocked to speak. The car was back in sight. But Jules was gone. 'Where?' stammered Shorty.

'My sister'.

Mark came to his senses. 'Get into the car'

'Shorty. I said get into the car!.'

'Get Aubry on the phone Paul.' His arm and head hurt but Mark managed to get the car started. All three men were hurt and shaken up. They tried to piece together all that had just happened. Aubry answered the phone. He had been waiting for them to call.

'What's happening there? The phone suddenly went silent.

Is everything ok?'

'No Aubry. We don't know what happened. Can you meet us somewhere?'

'Head back to the railway station. I'll meet there. And stay on the phone'. The drive was painfully silent. No one spoke. 'Where is Jules?' Shorty whispered in silence. Mark and Paul didn't know what to say. No

one knew what to do.

The sight of Aubry was the first bit of relief the men had. 'We need to get to a hospital. There is one up the road not too far from here' Aubry insisted as soon as he got into the car.

'Not till we have found Jules'.

Mark turned the car around and headed to the spot where they lost Jules.

The fog has cleared up. They looked frantically on the sides of the road for Jules. At a distance, Mark saw an object ahead of him. He slowed down and held his breath. Slowly they moved forward. In the middle of the road, battered and shaken, they found Jules tied to the end of a rope. Just as Shorty opened his door, Jules looked up at him and tried to reach out.

'Shorty, help!'.

Just then, the rope was tugged dragging Jules. Shorty looked in horror as his sister was dragged into the distance. Mark drove ahead and tried to keep Jules in sight. As they got closer, Jules was pulled further away from the car. For a moment, Jules looked into Mark's eye and cried for help.

'You've got to let her go. Don't go after her.' Aubry pleaded. 'That's my sister. We are not leaving her.' Shorty was never one to raise his voice or be assertive.

As the men chased Jules, a large castle revealed itself before them. The rope that Jules had been tied to, came all the way from the castle. Mark drove on.

'Not there, stop now.' Aubry was almost in tears. Jules went through the large gates and suddenly stopped and fell to the ground. Mark stopped the car, and the men ran out to Jules. Shorty picked up his sister and shook her.

'The blood of the innocent...' Boomed a loud noise from the castle. The stones of the castle shook with the voice. The three men looked up. This time, they could not see where the voice came from. They looked around and at the towering castle in front of them.

Mark heard the sound of the gates being slammed and turned around. Aubry hurriedly latched the gate.

'What are you doing Aubry?' Mark ran towards the gate.

'I begged you to stop. You did not listen. He knows you are here and now; I have no choice'. Whirlwinds of red dust erupted from the castle.

'The blood of the innocent will kill the man within' .

Chapter 3
Nathan

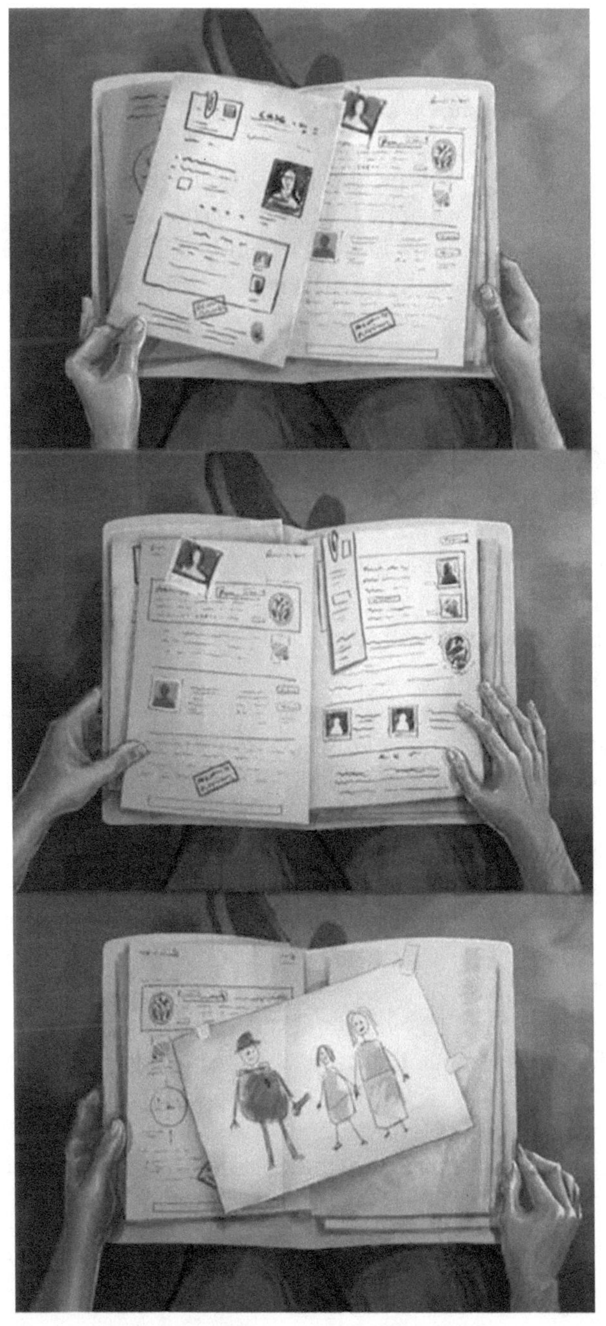

Present Day , Schwarzenberg

'Holly, that's a beautiful picture. But make my tummy smaller next time'.

Nathan smiled as he sipped his coffee. The children didn't complain when Nathan brought work home. But Holly did make it a point to make her presence felt occasionally by sneaking one of her drawings into Nathan's case files.

'You have to get rid of that broken mug Paapi'.

Eva has been trying to make breakfast for a while now. At 14, she decided to take charge of the kitchen and save herself and her little sister from her Paapi's dreadful cooking. She buttered the toast.

'The day you get out of college, pumpkin'.

Nathan tried to avoid the broken lip of his coffee mug. Getting up from the couch was more difficult than getting into it. Nathan began to look around for his walking stick.

'There you go. Now don't stay out too late, young man. The new nanny leaves at 6'.

Eva had taken charge of more than the kitchen. Nathan walked up to Holly. She cut a little heart out of paper and stuck it on her Paapi's jacket.

'You need more craft paper don't you Holly?'

Holly quickly nodded and smiled brightly.

Nathan grabbed his bag and walked out onto the street. Schwarzenberg didn't believe in waking up early. Nathan limped on. This leg never stopped him from walking to work every day. The street painter was priming his canvas.

'Not today old man'.

Every once in a while, Nathan picked up a painting from the old man. Not that he cared for paintings, but the chap could do with some spare change.

The police station at Schwarzenberg was housed in an old structure. Everything was retrofitted to turn the space into a functional police station.

'Easy on the sugar' he shouted to Burhman who was loading up his morning coffee.

'Been up all night.' Burhman massaged his belly. Nathan pulled himself into his desk.

'What have you been working on?"

Nathan attempted to clean the mess on his table like every morning and then, like every morning, gave up. Burhman sipped his coffee and a second later, pumped in more sugar. 'Drugs, trafficking, murder, theft… I've lost track Nathan'.

Burhman placed his coffee on top of a pile of files.

"Three months to retirement and I'll be sipping whiskey on my farm. Hope these cases don't kill me first.'

'Or the sugar in your coffee.'

'The Captain asked that this file be given to you.'

A uniformed officer Nathan had never seen in the station handed a beat-up file to Burhman.

Burhman ground his teeth and pulled on the file.

'No, no, not a chance. Not one more of these.'

'Nathan, can you take this case? I really can't have one more.' 'Nathan, meet the rookie. He has a name in there somewhere. Joined us yesterday. Hand over the file to Nathan there.'

'Heard about you at the academy. It's a pleasure to...'

'Then they told you the juvi story too? Quit the flattery. You don't report to me. Leave the file on the desk.'

'Easy there Nathan. Don't scare him on his first day here. Come on kid, I'll show you the town.' Burhman grabbed his coat and badge, patted the rookie on his shoulder and lead him out of the station.'

'Nathan is not too good with people. Especially new people. Takes his time.'

They got into Burhman's car. The rookie had to clear up the seat before he could sit down. Coffee cups, sandwich wrappers, files, bags. Burhman never believed in the litter box. The car pulled out of the parking lot.

'Nathan's had a rough life. And the force made it worse. He took on more than he could handle. Made enemies inside and outside of the force. Well, that's what you get for doing your job these days.'

'Family?' The rookie tried not to step on the juice boxes on the floor of the car.

Burhman felt like he had to explain Nathan to the rookie. As a consolation for the rudeness back at the station.

'Mother left when he was just 2. His father was a toner salesman who lived on the road mostly. She got sick of living on pennies. Nathan spent most of his childhood on the road with his father. And then the man went insane. That was rough on Nathan. His father would cover himself with toner ink and run around screaming. Poor kid spent four years living with the loon. Nathan wanted to be around Claire. This girl he grew up with. If the authorities found out about his father, Nathan would have to go to foster care and that meant moving away from Claire. But then, it finally happened. A teacher at his school found out and reported it.'

'The juvi story then?'

'Yes. That was another rough patch in his life. Nathan was a good kid. Kept to himself. Worked hard. But he had this thing for getting into trouble. Mostly for Claire. The girl stammered and got picked on in school. And Nathan could never tolerate that. So, you can imagine what he would do to a man who tried to get uncomfortably close to her.'

'You remember Theo Lauder, don't you?

'Claire's mother Louise worked as a trainee in his office. Now Louise was a wreck. Claire was the product of one of her drunken parties. Never knew who the father was. And Lauder, we all know Lauder. The day Lauder was appointed mayor, he went to celebrate with Louise. Now who would do that? Lauder used to have this special bring-your-child-to-work day only for Louise. And Lousie could do nothing about it.'

'So, Lauder lands up at her house with a bottle of wine. He sent Louise out to get some ice! Ice and wine! Poor Claire sat there helpless. The bastard! But Lauder had picked the wrong day. He had no idea Nathan was outside peeking through the window. He used to sneak in to meet her. The sight of Lauder's hand on Clair drove him mad. Nathan grabbed hold of a skillet and battered him. Lauder was hurt real bad, but managed to survive. Nathan was sent off to the Juvi. He never said a word about Claire. Nathan kept silent'.

'And the Juvi, we all know what that can do to a kid. He got beat up every single day. Till the day he fought back. And Nathan continued to fight. At 24, he was recruited into a unit called 'The Soulless'. A group of soldiers put together to do the government's dirty work. The bitterness and juvenile-home-infused-toughness are what the unit wanted. They don't even carry you back if you are wounded in an operation.

That's The Soulless.

Finally, when the unit was disbanded, Nathan was recruited onto the force. Impeccable record. Never took crap from anybody. The man once beat up a corrupt judge in court. He deserved that. But to beat up a judge? The system never forgets that. They tossed him around like salad. But could never break him.'

Back at the office, Nathan tried to make space on his desk to keep the file he was just handed. And not able to set it down anywhere, he decided to look through it.

Nino Accola, 21, had not returned home after he went trekking with his girlfriend to Werthenstein. Parents filed a missing person's complaint. Nathan took the file to the captain's office. 'I'll need to speak to the kid's parents'.

The captain didn't look up from the computer. 'Thought Burhman was looking into that case'.

'He asked me to take care of this one Capt. But why are we dealing with this case? Aren't we a little out of jurisdiction'?'

'The boy's father is an old colleague. He retired from our precinct. When the boy went missing, he came straight to me. I called the mountain police, but they never had a climb registered in either of the names. Makes that a problem the police need to deal with. And the station at Werthenstein is being wrapped up for some reason. We've been asked to step in.'

'This girl, Elsa Carli. Will need to speak to her family.' 'Do that and keep me posted, detective.'

The couple had been seeing each other for a few years. They shared their love of the outdoors. Nino Accola was an experienced climber and naturalist. Not some kid who'd get lost in the mountains. The Carli family lived in a small neighborhood two blocks from the station. Nathan rang the bell and waited for someone to open the door.

'Can I help you?'. A woman in her forties peeked through the gap in the door.

'The Carli family? I'm from the Schwarzenberg PD.' Before Nathan could pull out his badge, the woman at the door flung the door open like she had been waiting for him.

'Mrs. Carli?'

'No that's the maid Elena.' Adrian Carli stood at the end of the passage. 'Do come in'.

Elena showed Nathan into the living room. The walls were filled with pictures of Elsa from her trips around the world.

'I have a few questions that I hope you wouldn't mind answering.'

Mrs. Carli stormed into the room.

'Have you found our daughter? And the boy she was with?'

Mrs. Carli looked upset. And that, Nathan understood.

'This must be a difficult time for you. The department is trying its best.'

Nathan had just been assigned the case, but he had to say what he was trained to say.

'Tell me, after Elsa left on the 15th of November, has she ever contacted you? Sent you any pictures?'

'We're used to Elsa taking off on trips like these. She calls sometimes and maybe sends a picture or two. She normally has a bunch of friends. But ever since she met this boy, she's been going on climbs with him. We've met him a couple of times. She brought him home for dinner.'

Mrs. Carli sat annoyed and restless. 'Why do you make us repeat everything? The officer who came in first had the same questions to ask. And we have told him everything.' 'I've read the report Mrs. Carli. But as the detective assigned to this case, I've got to ask you the same questions. I'm sorry. Should I come back another day?'

'Might as well get this over with now'. Adrian Carli seemed to understand the situation much better. He wanted to cooperate.

'Mr. Carli, the department had the names of all of Elsa's friends and we've already contacted them. Is there anyone else you may have forgotten?

'We've always known all of Elsa's friends. Don't think there is anyone she has not told us about.'

Nathan got up to leave. 'Do let me know if you hear from someone. We'll continue with our investigation.' As he walked out, Elena came up to him and then stopped two steps short. She then walked away.

Back at the station Nathan sat at his desk going through Nino's and Elsa's social media accounts. A seasoned climber always registered with the Mountain Police. That was the rule. A uniformed officer walked in. 'There is a woman here to see you.'

Nathan looked across the hall and saw Elena. He always knew there was something she wanted to tell him. As Nathan approached her, she erupted.

'Sir, Miss Elsa… sir, she called. She pushed! Mrs. Carli knows'. Nathan calmed Elena down and got her a cup of coffee. 'Relax Elena, tell me all you know.'

'A couple of days after Miss Elsa went on that trip, she called Mrs. Carli on her phone. I was arranging her closet at the time. Miss Elsa was scared and crying. Mrs. Carli asked her to get back home. But the child never did. And Mrs. Carli isn't saying a word of that. Mrs. Carli asked me to leave the room and she shut the door in a hurry. I thought she'd mention the call to the police, but the madam has never uttered a word. Sir, I know something bad has happened. The child went missing after the call.'

'You can go back home Elena. And please act normal. We'll take it from here.'

'Bring her in for questioning, Nathan. Let's hear what she has to say. But do what you must do before that. And don't say a word to anyone about this. Captain Accola is a respectable man. Even after his service, the department looks up to him.' 'I get it, captain. Have asked for all the call records. Nino does not have a track record of crime. His friends and colleagues have only had good things to say about him. The couple have been going strong for some time now.'

Nathan tracked the phones. Elsa and Nino left Schwarzenberg on the 15th of November. After a couple of stops, they reached Werthenstein at nine in the evening. They seemed to have spent the evening at The White Crown Mountain Resort. Their movements were limited to the village on the 16th. On the 17th of November, the couple left the cabin towards the mountains. The last known position was about 12 miles east of the cabins. Nino's phone stayed at one location after 11 in that morning. Elsa's moved a couple of miles west and stopped. The phones were not traccable 12 hours after that. 'The batteries probably dried out' thought Nathan. And yes, Elena was right. The last call from Elsa's was to her mother. It lasted less than a minute.

The next day, Natan drove down to the Carli residence. Mrs. Carli would probably open up at home. Adrian Carli didn't seem too happy to see Nathan again. The repeated questioning turned out to be an inconvenience.

'I need to speak to Mrs. Carli.'

Nathan did not waste time. Adrian was irritated this time. His wife was already going through a lot.

'And what new question do you have for her?'

'Why your daughter contacted her from Werthenstein!'

'She told you yesterday. There was just one call.'

'That's before I went through the call records. Mr. Carli, your wife is hiding something, and I need to know what it is. Or do you want me to call her into the station for questioning?' Nathan was getting aggressive as well.

'She didn't mean do it'. Mrs. Carli's weak voice muffled with sobbing came from the living room.

'Didn't do what? What are you talking about Marsha?'

Adrian was shocked.

'Mrs. Carli, you need to tell me what you know.'

Marsha Carli broke down. The feelings she had been suppressing for days, came out that instant. She cried for a while and then regained her composure, ready to talk.

Adrian Carli was confused and upset.

'Elsa called me. She was crying, shivering, in a frenzy. Nino tried to attack her in the mountains. As she tried to get away, she pushed him into a deep cavern. She didn't mean to kill him. My poor child was trying to protect herself. I asked her to come home right away. But she never did. She is probably hiding. She didn't mean to kill him.'

She continued to cry.

'Mrs. Carli, we don't know if anyone is dead. All we know now is that they are missing. Had you told us about this in the beginning of the investigation, we wouldn't have lost all this time.'

What started as a man missing case had turned into a possible murder. Nathan tried to join the dots in his mind. Nino Accola had clean records. No reported crime. No reports of drug use or alcoholism. And why would he try to kill Elsa? No one would plan a murder on such a trail. Something had happened in Werthenstein.

Nathan met the Captain to brief him on the new developments.

'Let's not tell the Accolas anything about this till we have more information on Nathan. It's too soon to say anything.'

'Do you think you can get the Werthenstein police to assist us, Captain?'

'I can call the captain there. They are not going to be of much help. It's a small station.'

'You make your call. I'll head there in the morning, Captain.'

On the way to Werthenstein, Natan made stops at a couple of filling stations and cafes. One of the waiters remembered the couple. They had stopped there for lunch. The waiter did not remember anything odd about them.

Werthenstein was a quiet little place. And the police station, quieter. So quiet you could hear the hum of the computers. Nathan hadn't seen a messier station. Files piled on desks, open take-out containers and that's it. There was nobody at the station. He walked around looking for the captain's office. Nathan found the closed cabin door a little amusing.

The station was literally empty! Nathan knocked. 'Yes, Freston. What is it this time?'

'I'm from Schwarzenberg. We've been given the case of the missing trekkers. And who is Freston?' Nathan didn't see anyone on his way in.

'Didn't expect them to send someone in so fast'

'Freston!' 'No, Nathan.'

'No, not you. Freston, get in here.'

The captain sat in a cabin that was tidier by the standards of the rest of the police station. 'Yes. That case. As you can seem we've been asked to wind up operations. My officers have been transferred out. Freston and I have stayed on to pack up. Freston helps with the paperwork. New kid.'

'Not of much use, but he is all I got.'

'Why would the department wrap up a station?'

'Budget cuts I presume'. The captain seemed quite clueless.

Freston walked into the cabin peeking up from the frame of his glasses. His oversized clothes covered a skinny frame. Freston was more suited to working in a bank. Or an accountant's office. Never a police station.

'Can you help the detective with the details on the Accola Carli case Freston?'

Nathan followed Freston out of the captain's cabin.

'I've not been here long. Just getting to know this place better.'

The hem of his saggy pants wiped the floor as he walked. 'I can show you a few things the detective left behind.'

Freston handed Nathan a box with a few files and headed back to the filing he was doing before the captain called him.

Nathan sat down between the mess and began going through the files.

'This case file I've been given is more like a child's book report. Is this all the detective managed to collect on this case?' Nathan looked patiently as Freston tried to punch filling holes with a pen.

'That's all we have.'

'Do you know anything about this resort called The White Crown?'

'No, like I said, just got here. Getting to know the place.'

Nathan wasn't about to get any help from this station. As he walked out, Freston accidentally pulled open the cover of a paper punch flooding his desk with little paper circles. The police department was desperate for office staff, and they had decided to lower their non-existent recruitment standards.

The White Crown was about two miles from the station. Everything in Werthenstein was a short drive from everything else. The White Crown was a broken-down old place. The doors hung loose, and the windows had metal sheets hammered on in the place of glass. The reception had a board on with a few letters missing. Nathan looked over the counter. A man sat warming his hands over a small room heater.

'We only take cash; the machine is broken. Full payment up front or get out.'

'I'm not looking for a room. I'm from the police department. Have a few questions about a couple of trekkers who stayed here.'

'Who are you looking for?'

'Nino Accola, Elsa Carli. They were here on the 17th of March.'

'Those damn kids owe me money. Left without paying. If you find them, you'd better get back my money.'

'Tell me. Did you notice anything peculiar about them? Any arguments? Fights? Did they seem happy?'

'I run an establishment here. Not a kissing booth. How'd I know what these kids are up to. These kids and their damn fantasies. They come here for their Instabooks and Facegrams. Many leave without paying me the balance. Crazy generation. They go looking for ghosts in the mountains and dragons in the valley. This internet thing makes everyone go mad. Dragons and ghosts!'

'Can you show me to the cabin they stayed in?' 'Cabin 18. The last one there.'

The manager got up to give Nathan the key.

'They didn't leave anything behind. Wish they had. Would have taken care of the rent. Damn vagabonds. Didn't have a thing of value.'

The chap was right. Nino and Elsa had packed everything before they left. But would have definitely planned on returning. Both of them didn't seem the type that would run off without paying the rent. Nathan set off on the track the couple had.

Every climber and had to be cleared by the mountain police before they set off on a trail. There was also a deposit to be paid. Most professionals and seasoned trekkers followed the rules in the interest of their own safety. But every once in a while; there were a few who just wandered in. And unfortunately, these were the most reckless.

Nathan reached the spot. He got out of his car and walked around. The land was flat and covered with about 6 inches of snow. There were no crevices in sight. And besides, this didn't seem like a place that could have a crevice or fissures on land. It was mostly flat. Elsa's call didn't make any sense now. The cell phone trail had ended here and this was probably the place where Nino attacked Elsa. But the crevice she claimed to have pushed Nino into was not here. Something like that does not get covered up by snow.

Mrs. Carli could have misled him, but the mobile signal trail could never have gone wrong. As Nathan stood wondering, fog began to form around him. He had to drive back before he lost visibility. Back at the Werthenstein station, Freston cleared a table that Nathan could use as a temporary workstation.

'Are you planning to head back to Schwarzenberg today, detective?'

'I do intend to.' Nathan had to get back to the kids.

'But there has been a snowslide on Route 10. They'll take a day to clear it. Looks like you're stuck here for the night.' 'Damn. I wanted to get back to my kids. Is there a place I can stay?'

'You'll need to check with the Captain.'

Nathan called Burhman. 'Need you to do me a favor. I'm stuck in Werthenstein. Can you and Gennie take care of the kids tonight?'

Burhman was glad to help. That's the least he could do for Nathan.

'The White Crown is all we've got here.'

The captain empathized with Nathan. Everyone knew it was a dump. Nathan was never into anything fancy. He led a simple life. All he wanted was a bed and a place to shower. And that, The White Crown had.

Back at the resort, Nathan found the manager in the same place he had left him. And when he heard the door open, he delivered his usual line.

'Now, what would you like to know now?' He was hoping for a guest.

'I'd actually like a cabin.'

'A cabin with the view of the mountains or the view of the road?'

'A cabin with a door preferably. Anything basic and inexpensive. And yes, hot water'.

'We have 2 cabins in the economy range. One does not have hot water. The other has hot water, but the mattress has holes in it. What would you like?'

Nathan paid the manager and walked towards his cabin. 'You'll find a locked cellar there. I keep my stuff in there.'

The manager was counting his money over and over again. The cabin was good enough to spend the night. The last cleaning it got was after it was built.

The nights in Werthenstein were darker than any place. Like a quiet town should be. The population was slim and so were the streetlights. Natan had a quick dinner from a restaurant near the resort and called home to check on the kids. Eva wasn't pleased that father wasn't coming home to tuck in her little sister. She spoke for Holly. The children had never stayed away from Nathan. Nathan cursed the snowslide and the roads that people built close to mountains.

Back in the cabin, he stood in the shower nursing his leg with hot water. He never let the leg affect his work, but at night, after the distraction of work, the leg reminded him of his neglect. As he laid down to sleep, he thought of the children. He knew Eva would tuck Holly into bed. He was proud of the children he had raised. Nathan dosed off.

'Yajamanasya Swagathamasthi'

Nathan heard the words. He didn't know what it meant.

'Yajamanasya Swagathamasthi'

He heard it again. Louder. Nathan opened his eyes to see himself suspended by the waist from a long rope. He hung from the finger of a figure larger than him. Much larger. His back hurt. The rope began to rock sideways like a pendulum.

'Yajamanasya Swagathamasthi'

The voice above him boomed. Nathan lost his breath and jumped up from his mattress sweating. A dream had never felt that real. Nathan sat gasping for air. Sweating profusely. His mouth ran dry. He grabbed the glass of water that was handed to him and drank it in a hurry. As he reached the bottom of the glass, reality began to dawn on him.

Where did the glass of water come from?

Nathan rolled off the mattress to see a woman standing by his bed. Dressed in tattered clothes. Slowly and softly, she began to chant.

'Swami Daasa Bhavathi. Daasarshy Swami Bhavathi' *'Swami Daasa Bhavathi. Daasarshy Swami Bhavathi'*

Nathan sprang up. 'How did you get in? Who are you?' He could not see the woman's face in the darkness. Nathan moved away from the bed looking for his gun. The woman stood still.

'Swami Daasa Bhavathi. Daasarshy Swami Bhavathi'

That's all she said. Nathan grabbed hold of the bedsheet and tied up the woman and turned on the light. Her face was bruised and covered with dirt, but from the picture he had seen, he could recognize Elsa Carli. She did not resist. Her arms and face were covered in strange markings. Some strange language. None of her records mentioned any tattoos or piercings.

Nathan pulled Elsa into his car. She sat expressionless. Driving to the station, Nathan asked her about Nino, but he did not get a reply.

At the station, Freston and the Captain were playing cards on a stack of boxes. 'Hand me the keys to the cell.' Nathan shouted as he led lifeless Elsa. Freston and the Captain ran up to him with the keys.

'That's the safest place for her. She made it to my room somehow. She is delirious. We need to get her to a doctor.'

'At this time of the night? There is a vet not too far from here.' Freston knew something about the town and even that was useless information.

'Who is this, Nathan?'

'Elsa Carli. The girl I have been looking for.'

The rest of the night, Nathan could not sleep. He sat by the cell looking at Elsa who didn't bat an eyelid. She sat without saying a word.

In the morning, Freston made coffee for everyone. Now there was something he was good at. Nathan heard a car drive up outside the station as he was heading out to look for a doctor. Holly and Eva ran out of the car. They hugged their father.

'Holly ran out of her bed screaming in the middle of the night. She cried through the night. I brought her here as soon as we saw light.'

Burhman looked worried as he got out of the car. Nathan hugged his daughters.

'It must have been a bad dream child. Just a bad dream.' We'll go to the cottage. Let's take my car.'

Holly refused to let go of him as he sat her down in the rear seat.

'Burhman, can you drive? I'll give you directions.'

Holly had fallen asleep by the time they got to the cottage. Nathan lay her on the bed being careful not to wake her up. Nathan and Burhman sat by the fire. Nothing that had happened over the past couple of days made any sense to Nathan, but he tried to explain it to Burhman.

'Paapi, we've left Holly's medicines at home. She will need her medicines.'

'Let's head home, Burhman.' Nathan grabbed his keys and ran towards the room with Holly.

'I'll call up the station and let them know.' Nathan dialed the station. Freston answered.

'Freston, we need to go to Schwarzenberg for a bit. I should be back soon.'

'Detective, there has been a landslide on the road leading into town. I'm afraid you cannot drive through. The captain and I are heading out to put up signs on the road.'

'I need to reach Schwarzenberg as soon as possible. Put the Captain on the phone.'

'Captain, is there any way I can get out of town. It's an emergency.

I need to get Holly and Eva home.'

The captain was silent for a few seconds. 'Captain!'

'There is one way. We have a snowmobile at the precinct that you could drive to the closest highway. And then probably hitch a hike from there. But you cannot take the kids on it. It's too dangerous.'

'I'll probably head home and get the medicine then.' 'Burhman, be here with the kids. I'll try and be back as soon as possible.'

Nathan drove to the station and found the snowmobile in the garage. As

the captain had suggested, he found his way to the closest highway and hitched a ride home.

It was only on the drive home that Natan got a chance to get his thoughts together. The chaos and panic had left him doing things without thinking. He was reacting to situations, not thinking things through. Did he have to leave the children at Werthenstein? Was there something else he could have done?

Nathan rushed through the front door into Holly's room. The room was always colorful. Holly loved to make little things out of paper. Her little pieces of art often spoke for her. They were the only means by which she could express herself. Nathan looked around for the box of medicines. Eva had always been careful about where she kept the medicines.

At the far corner of the room, Nathan saw something that was nothing like the regular paintings, paper animals and stars that filled her room. Human figurines made of paper, hung from pieces of red string. From the waist. Nathan could feel blood rush into his eyes. He began to shiver. Nothing ever scared Nathan, but this was more than he could handle.

His daughter was a part of everything he was going through. Nathan called Burhman and asked to speak with Eva.

'Listen to me carefully, what has Holly been doing the past few days? What has she seen? Has she been reading anything or speaking to anyone else?'

Nathan tried hard not to scare Eva.

'Holly went into your room looking for craft paper. She was rummaging through your drawer.'

Nathan entered his room to find the cupboards open. Holly had looked through a lot of stuff he had kept away from the children. Medical records of his father, pictures, and recordings from the hospital during his treatment. Why would Holly do this?. As he arranged the pictures back into the folder, one caught his attention- A photograph of his father in the asylum cell. Covered in toner ink. This is a picture Nathan had seen before, but this time he noticed something new. The markings all over the cell walls looked a lot like the ones he had seen on Elsa the night before. They were the same. And around the markings, were drawings of figures hanging by the waist. Nathan went blank. Cluelessness has an effect on the body. It renders one numb.

His hands searched for a video tape once seen amongst the files. Nathan had kept away from his father's medical records. He always wanted to forget that part of his life. But today, destiny wanted him to face his past. He pushed the tape into an old cassette player. Nathan never liked to throw away old things. Curled up in the corner of the cell, his father sat repeating something. Something Nathan had never paid attention to before.

'Swami Daasa Bhavathi. Daasrshy Swami Bhavathi.' 'Swami Daasa Bhavathi. Daasrshy Swami Bhavathi.'

The foreign words that he had heard Elsa say. He could not understand the meaning of the words. But what his father said with fear, Elsa chanted without expression.

Nathan had lost all the energy to ask questions in his mind. He sat looking at the screen as it played on. A few minutes later, the situation he was in, hit him hard. He stood up realizing that there was not a lot of time to lose. To make sense of the situation and attach logic to it, that had to be done another day.

With a mind in chaos, he called the station. He didn't know how he could make the Captain understand. No one answered. Before he could cut the call, the new rookie answered. 'I need to speak to the captain. This is Nathan.'

'The captain is at central. Is there anything I can help you with Detective?'

The rookie was looking for a way to make up for the bad impression the previous day.

'I'm sending you a few pictures. Run a search on the international database. And see if you can dig up any information on Werthenstein. Anything you can. And how soon can you meet me at my place?'

He knew the rookie would not ask too many questions. And when he did not have any answers, someone like this was best. Natan hung up and called Burhman to check on the children.

'They are fine, when are you back?'

'I'll be back soon. Something has come up.'

Nathan didn't want to get Burman worried. If the children had to remain calm, so did Burhman. An hour went by. Nathan was composed now. Nervous, but composed. The doorbell rang.

'Detective, got here as soon as I could get the data you asked for.'

Impatiently, Nathan grabbed the folder from the rookie.

'Over the past few years, we have had quite a few people go missing in and around Werthenstein. Mostly reported as lost in the mountains. Some lost on the way. No bodies found. Nathan looked through the photographs. And he stopped at one. Someone who looked very familiar. A man he had seen every day.

The rookie continued to talk. But Nathan did not hear a word. He kept staring at the photograph.

'I have seen this man. I know this man.' The painter Nathan walked past every day. 'I know where to find him.'

Nathan and the rookie drove to the spot where the painter normally set shop. The spot was empty.

'If you're looking for the painter, he's at the community soup kitchen.' The newsstand owner shouted across the street. 'Who are we looking for, Detective?' The rookie was careful with his questions. He did not know what mood he was in.

'There is this painter I walk past every day. I've brought a couple of his paintings. Just to help out the poor guy. I saw his photograph in the file you brought.

A bit older, but it's definitely him.'

'But the database has marked him as missing.

He went missing 5 years ago. Never found.'

'I know it's him. Can't be a resemblance.'

People were just queuing up at the soup kitchen. And at the end of the street, Nathan found the painter silently sipping his meal.

'Is your name Liam?'

'I've not been called that in years. Who are you? The painter paused at the mention of his name.

'You have been reported missing. Where have you been?' Nathan kneeled by the man.

'You walk by me every day, don't you. I recognize the sound of the cane. The man with you, can you send him to buy me a sandwich? I've been drinking the same soup for several days now.'

Nathan looked up at the rookie who was more than eager to run to the sandwich shop. He helped Liam off the ground and onto a bench nearby.

'What happened to you in Werthenstein?'

'I can smell the mountain air in your clothes. You have been there too. I've been trying to forget Werthenstein. Many years ago, I went there to paint the landscape. But those mountains were not kind to me. I was not born blind. They gouged out my eyes.'

'They? Who did this to you?'

'I was abducted from my tent one night. Gagged and blind folded. I never saw a thing. They took me some place I don't know. I heard chanting in a foreign language. I remember cold stone walls and floors. I remember everything I could feel with my arms. I was left in a large hall in the company of this old man who told me stories - Stories of a beast.'

'Can you tell me anything about the kidnapers? Were there more people like you?'

'I never saw anyone and after I lost my eyes, it was just darkness and voices. The only person who spoke to me was this old man. Perhaps kept captive there as well. Maybe his story has something in it that you may want.' At first, I thought it was a mad man's story, but after living through the atmosphere of the place, I learned to believe in it.'

Strange things had happened over the past few days. Nathan was prepared for more.

Liam took a deep breath.

Chapter 4
Birth

Man has had a relationship with gold like no other metal. As he got closer to it, he strayed away from everything else.

Stories from the east have always enthralled the world. But this was not just a story. This is a witness account. The witness, the only voice that spoke to Liam.

In the tip of Peninsular India, stood a mountain range that hid a small province, *Parashunaadu* believed to be under the protection of the reigning deity. *Parashunaadu*, worshiped and credited all its glory to the Deva of the *Gajakeshava* Temple. The happiness and peace that the people enjoyed was by the grace of the Deva. But not everyone came to the temple to experience its divinity. The temple concealed within its vaults, the glory of *Parashunaadu*, the gold of the deva and the pride of every man woman and child. And the men who were drawn to its luster, had to answer to the forest that guarded the temple.

On a moonless cold night, three men ascended the cliff by the temple to access the vault. Crafty little men who hung by ropes tied to the bellies of large monitor lizards. Crafty and silent men, who took pride in their stealthiness. Crafty men who couldn't predict what they were about to face. Placing two of his friends outside the cave, the lockpicker made his way in. The entranceway to the vault door was covered with paintings. And at the end, the stone door with three keyholes.

By the light of his lamp, Devabrahma Devanaar sat with his legs crossed, deep in meditation. The locksmith pulled out his picking tools from a small pouch and holding his breath inserted it slowly into one of the keyholes. And at that very moment, Devabrahma broke out of his meditative state and uttered the name of his lord in shock. He had sensed the breach in the temple he served. Devabrahma walked out of his house with a lamp to light his path.

The locksmith took a second breath and inserted a second picking tool trying to feel the internal mechanism of the lock. He felt the door rumbling and as he got closer to the door to put his ears against it, spikes sprang out from the walls around him. The men who stood watch were lifted by their feet and it was only when they were up in the air that they realized that they were hanging upside down from the trunks of elephants. The elephants were about to throw the men to the ground.

'Nigrah' Came a human voice between the trumpets of the elephants. The spikes stopped short of the lockpicker's eyes and body. Short enough

that he could feel the cold in the metal. The locksmith fell to the ground, got up and ran out of the cave. At its entrance, he saw the elephants stand in a circle. His companions were on the ground shocked more than he was.

Amongst the elephants, stood a man with a lamp in his hands.

'And you thought you could walk away with the Deva's treasure? I spared your blood today to protect the sanctity of this soil. The Deva's treasure will stay in the vaults of the temple as long as the forest and its creatures stand guard and till my last breath. I, Sarvagyani Devabrama Devanaar, priest of the Gajakeshava Temple and keeper of all its secrets.'

The forest echoed the priest's voice as if it agreed with him.

The next morning, the markets, and streets of *Parashunaadu* saw a sight they had grown accustomed to seeing. The outsiders, however, stood with their mouths open as the elephants carried the thieves to the house of the *Naaduvaazi,* the chieftain for judgement. The Kevoor family had held the title of *Naaduvaazi* for over eight generations. Their word was the law, and they answered only to the King of the land. Kevoor Shakthinarayanan Thambi, the current *Naaduvaazi* looked down at the scrawny bodies of the thieves.

'Subra, the stories of our land seem to have reached other shores.'

Subra fanned the *Naaduvaazi* and smiled.

'I gather you animals have heard of the gold, but not of the forest that protects it.'

'And never of a man who could command the forest *Umbra.*' One of the thieves whispered without looking up.

'Subra, show our visitors around the village. Tell them of our ways and teach them well.'

As the Naaduvaazi walked away, he pulled Subran towards him and whispered.

'And learn what you can from them.'

The wheels of the bullock cart climbed over the rocks on the road. Subra cracked his whip and fed grass to the bullocks that sat behind him.

'Pull dogs, Pull'

He shouted as he flogged the three men who pulled the cart.

'Which one of you three dogs is the lock picker?' 'Me Umbra.'

'Step aside and walk with me.'

The locksmith walked by the cart rubbing his bruised arms. The other two men struggled down the road.

'A lockpicker is an artist with hands too tender to pull a cart. We'll leave that to the animals. Are you any good at your craft?'

'There has never been a lock I could not pick Umbra.'

'And the lock at the temple, was that not a real lock?' Subran mocked.

'There is magic in that lock Umbra. I've never seen anything like that. Three locks that work in some kind of combination. And the wrong combination sets off a trap. I'd have been shredded if the priest hadn't gotten there on time.'

'Tell me about the locks.'

'Two of them Umbra, have carvings of frogs on them and one has a bird. The keyholes, unlike any I've seen are just slits.'

'Maybe it's time for you to join your friends.'

Subran had wished for more information, but this is all the men knew. Back at the *Naaduvaazi's* residence, the bullocks chewed on fresh grass.

'Melore Velia Tachan. The incarnation of Lord Vishwakarma himself! The architect of the Gajakeshava Temple. That vault is his greatest masterpiece. Commissioned by my grand uncle Kevoor Sadashivan Thambi. The generous fool. Gave away all the family wealth to the temple.'

The *Naaduvaazi's* eyes shot up with blood and he ground his teeth as he mentioned the name of his grand uncle.

'And the temple honors our family with a title in return. An entitlement to hold court for these savages. And as I tackle moneylenders, the gold that is rightfully mine lies in the vaults. All the property of a deity. What good is gold to the gods?'

'Is that all you could gather from the thieves, Subra? This is the first time someone has managed to get past the elephants to the vault door.'

'Thats all he saw *Umbra*.' Subran mixed the feed for the cattle. The Naaduvaazi stood up from the heap of jute bags he had been sitting on. 'We need to find a way inside the vault.'

'What do we do with them?' Subran kicked the jute bags the Naaduvaazi had been sitting on.

'Have you shown them the river, Subra?'

'It's as simple as this. You fold in this part and you pull on these two.'

Devabrahma placed the bird he had made of palm leaves into Daathi's little hands. Her eyes lit up and she smiled brightly.

'I've been trying to make these for days. You do have magic in your finger's Vishnu's *achha*. I wish my *achhan* was more like you.'

Daathi looked at the bird in wonder.

'Your father Daathi Kutty, is the *Naaduvaazi* of this land. A man respected by everyone. He has responsibilities that are very important. Besides, I'm here to make you all the birds you need.'

'Yes Daathi, my *achhan* will make you all the birds you need. Here, I made you little earrings with the leaf. You can wear it to the *Thiruviza*.' Vishnu looped the palm leaf earrings around Daathi's ears, and she chuckled with happiness.

'I've also got something you like Daathi Kutty. I just made these.' Maya walked in with a brass plate filled with *Neiappams*. Daathi ran to her.

'Vishnu's Amma, you make the best *Neiappams* in the whole of Parashunaadu. In the next life I wish to be born as your daughter.'

'Daathi Kutty, we have watched you grow with Vishnu. You will always be like a daughter to us. You really don't have to wait for the next life. Enjoy you *Neiapppams* and practice making those birds.'

The door at the entrance swung open. Birds around the house stopped chirping.

'The village talks of the priest who saved the Deva's wealth!' Kethaki stepped in. His long locks were covered in thin strips of golden metal and body covered with red markings. The sight of the man scared Daathi and she ran to hide behind Maya. Kethaki had his son Karshanya with him. A smaller version of the man himself.

"Humor me, priest. How different is your magic from mine? The magic that you despise so much. The magic you campaign to put an end to.' The silence in nature, when Kethaki spoke, was unsettling. But Devabrahma feared no one.

'The difference Kethaki? All you seek is to control and steer the forces you can never fully understand. The *Rudragni* that you claim to have harnessed, you use like a toy. And I, I am no *Manthravaadi*. Just an instrument through which the *Deva* works.'

This was not the first time Devabrahma tried to explain to Kethaki, but he tried anyway. The battle of words and magic was an old one that dated back several generations. The Devannars and the Thamoprabhus never agreed with each other.

Kethaki turned around to leave and gestured Karshanya to follow. 'One day, priest, you will understand what it means to control the dark forces. And then your family will pay the price for the centuries of contempt. And while in the subject of toys…' Kethaki rose his fingers and waved a sign in air. The palm leaf birds around the children began to move and they rose up in the air circling Daathi and Vishnu. The children looked up in wonder. Devabrahma clenched his fist.

'How dare you Kethaki! You have the audacity to cast spells in my *Illam*. Forces of nature you play with are not yours to command.'

Maya had never seen her husband raise his voice. And when Devabrahma spoke, even Kethaki showed signs of fear.

The birds in the air fell to the ground and burnt to ashes. Kethaki looked back from his shoulders and whispered in fury **'Time will give me the reigns, Priest.'**

And as Kethaki walked away, every blade of grass he stepped on, burned to dust.

The sickles tore through the sheaves of paddy. With arms tied behind his back, the Naaduvaazi looked on, furious and irritated with the sound the tool made when it cut through the paddy in his fields.

'How many years Subra?'

Subran hesitated and looked down. 'Five Umbra.'

'For five years, I have to watch these moneylenders take away the harvest from my fields. The Naaduvazhi does not have authority of his own soil?' The Naaduvazhi watched as the workers carried away bundle after bundle of paddy. 'The villagers should never know this.'

'Do not worry Umbra, not even the workers know. But Umbra, the harvest does not even account for half of what you owe them.'

Subran spoke with caution. He had to remind his *Thampuran* of the condition he was in.

'Subra, my family's wealth lies in the temple vault. Unused. Ceremonial. I want it. What is the use of this title I hold if I have to plead with moneylenders for time?'

'Umbra, the priest guards the temples with his elephants and even if we make it past them, we have to deal with a vault door protected with magic. We have secretly had so many men try to get in. And not one, has even managed to see the gold.

'But there is one man who can help us.' The Naaduvaazi whispered.

'Ketaki'

As the Naaduvaazi said the name, fear began creeping up his body. The daring and bold *Naaduvaazi* of Parashunaadu feared only one man just as every other ordinary man. The thought of being in the presence of the darkest soul in all land made him sweat.

The scrawny trees wound like the fingers on a beggar's hands. Standing up against the darkness that was neither blue nor black. If one looked carefully at the trees, they moved with intent. So, Subra decided to look straight on towards the path that his torch lit.

'Must we travel at night *Umbra*? And that too to Ketaki's *Manthrashaala*?'

'I can't be seen visiting Kethaki during the day. And what are you afraid of Subra? The ghost of your second wife you strangled to death.'

Subran shyly scratched his head. 'That was my first wife *Umbra*.'

As they got closer to the *Manthrashaala*, Subran looked up to see red strings tied around the trees. Black bags hung from them. Chanting could be heard at a distance. And in between the chanting came snarls of animals.

'Hold the torch forward Subra.'

The light of the torch fell on two figures chained to the trees. They appeared to stand guard. Subran went closer. He waved the torch to make it burn brighter. In the light, the Naaduvaazi saw two men in chains. Sitting on all fours. The men snarled and barked at Subran.

'Put out the fire and enter Subra. You are scaring them.'

A voice from a distance. The men could not see the speaker.

Two large trees with figures carved into them arched on one another to form the entrance into Kethaki's *Manthrashaala.*

'Naaduvaazi, two thieves tried to steal from me last week. That's when I realized that I needed guard dogs.'

Subran looked back at the men at the entrance. They barked. Subran looked away.

The Naaduvaazi saw a fire burn at a distance. That is where the voice came from. The men walked slowly dragging their feet. The path was canopied by trees without leaves or any sign of life. They were dabbed with red paste. Stone figurines clung onto the trees.

The fire in Kethaki's altar burned high. When Subran looked into them carefully, he spotted figures of demons in the fire. They roared as the fire raged. Subran shivered. Kethaki's eyes were closed. He ripped out a lock of hair from behind him and threw it into the fire along with the metal piece strung to it. The fire flared up.

'The Naaduvaazi of Parashunaadu in Kethaki's *Manthrashaala,* the very land your people call cursed. This visit must be backed with serious intention. How can Kethaki be of service to the Naaduvaazi?'

'I am not here to discuss that Kethaki. Say I have use for your magic. What would you want in return?'

The Naaduvaazi stood firm.

'My Magic Naaduvaazi, cannot end your gambling debt. So that is not what brings you here. And money, you do not seek to borrow from a man like me. Aah yes, the Deva's gold. Now, not even my spells can break through the vault doors of the temple.'

'How…how?' The Naaduvaazi shuddered. Not even his wife knew of the gambling debts he had amassed. And the gold, only Subran knew about it.

'What surprises you Naaduvaazi? The fact that you underestimated me or the fact that there is nothing I don't know? *Naaduvaazi,* **I am Irulnaadha Thamoprabhu Kethaki**. What I can see in the darkness, men cannot see in the light. And secrets, don't they hide in the darkness?' Kethaki's eyes remained shut.

He continued. 'But the vaults, they are beyond what even I can do. They are protected by the keys forged in the *Devagni.'*

Subran flexed his chest 'what if I got the keys from the puny priest?'

'What you possess in size Subra, you lack in intellect. You think it's that simple? The keys are only one half of your problem. They need to be used in a sequence. And that sequence is hidden in a verse that has been handed down the bloodline of the Devanaar Clan. From father to son only at the deathbed. It's not written down anywhere. And nobody outside the family has heard it. The powers that Devabrahma commands stem from the secrets that he protects. You need more than the strength of iron and muscle to get into that vault. You need the priest himself.'

The night was long. Longer than all the other nights for the Naaduvaazi. That night, he had to craft a plan to do the impossible.

'Vishnu, you are getting heavier. You do know that?' 'Acha, get on with your story.'

'And as I was saying. God made man out of clay. To harden the clay, he baked it in the Divine *Devaagni*. The fire which gave life. And that man, was put on earth to care for its creatures, its flowers, trees and mountains. But man perished on earth. He was no match for the animals that roamed the earth, the rains and the storms. And that is when God began to bake his clay figures in a mix of *Devaagni* and the *Rudragni*. In the right quantity, the *Rudragni* gave man his strength and virility. It gave him what he needed to survive the harshness of earth. As the fires baked the clay, the God of Wind blows between them causing them to burn in patterns not predictable. If the God of Wind chose to blow stronger in one direction, the man thus formed, turned out to be more aggressive. If it chose to blow in another, the man would become timid. And thus, was formed mankind where no man was alike.'

Devabrahma carried Vishnu up the steps that lead to the Gajakeshava Temple like every other day. The father and son, both enjoyed these climbs, but there was something else that Vishnu was truly looking forward to.

'Faster *Achha,* Sudeendra must be waiting for me. I have this large ball of jaggery for him today. He is going to be thrilled.'

As Devabrahma walked in through the entrance, Sudeendra trumpeted. Vishnu was right. Sudeendra picked Vishnu up from Devabrahma's back and placed him on his. Vishnu hugged the elephant and eagerly pushed the ball of jaggery into its curled-up truck. Sudeendra shook from side to side in excitement. He loved Vishnu.

Devabrahma bathed in the temple pond and prepared for the morning rituals. As he entered the sanatorium, the elephants lit the lamps on the pillars. The statue of the Deva on the eagle began to glow in the light of the lamps. Seeing this, a tear rolled down Devabrahma's eyes. He prostrated in front of the idol in devotion.

'Deva, I am truly blessed to be witness to your radiance. Bless me Oh Lord so that I and my son after me, can be in your service. You, the benevolent one, appeased by even the smallest offerings from your devotees, pray, shine upon me.'

That was the effect the idol had the first time Devabrahma saw it as a child. That was the effect the idol had every day that Devabrahma saw it.

Vishnu entered hanging onto Sudeendra's trunk.

'*Achha*, do come home early this evening, you have to take *Amma* and me to the *Thiruviza*. 'Sudeendra, I'll bring back puffed rice for you. Daathi kutty will be there. I'll be seeing the *Paavakoothu* with her. You will not understand the *Paavakoothu*, so you stay with the Deva.'

The *Thiruviza* was a yearly harvest festival in Parashunaadu. Traders flocked to its markets, entertainers and showmen set up stage. Children and grownups alike waited for the *Thiruvizha*. And the Naaduvaazi along with the temple council, on this auspicious day would plan the rituals to be carried out in the year to come.

'Go ahead Maya, do buy those red bangles. They will look good around your wrist.'

All Maya liked to do was look through the stalls of the *Thiruvizha*. She never wanted to spend her husband's humble earnings on color and glitter. But Devabrahma knew that even something as simple as glass bangles would bring great joy to Maya. And he lived to see that happiness.

'*Amma, Achaa*, I'm going to find Daathi. We'll watch the *Paavakooth* together. You will be busy with the council and the Naaduvaazi.' Vishnu ran into the crowd.

The villagers gathered around the central stage. The temple council walked in followed by the Naaduvaazi. And then, Devabrahma.

The Naaduvaazi stood up to address the gathering.

'Subjects, the glory of Parashunaadu is the radiance of the Deva that protects it. This year, our harvest has been scanty. Locusts and pests have infested our crops. I have with me the temple astrologer who tells me that the Deva is not pleased. I ask the council for recommendations. What should we do?'

This is not what Devabrahma expected. He shared a bond with the Divine Deva. If the Deva was displeased, he would have sensed it. But Devabrahma knew he was not to interrupt the Naaduvaazi.

'We would like to call for a *Devapreethi Maha Yaagam* to appease the Deva. The largest Yaaga ever conducted. A twelve-day Yaaga to be conducted under the guidance of a *Yaagaacharya*.' The oldest of the council members got up and announced.

'The Council only suggests whats best for the people. I think we should go ahead with the Yaagam.' The Naaduvaazhi announced.

'Who would be ideal as the *Yaagaacharya*?' The second council member got up to speak.

'Someone with the knowledge of all the scriptures, a scholar in all the spiritual languages.'

'Well, there is only one such man in the whole of Parashunaadu. Sarvagyani Devabrahma Devanaar. The head priest of the Gajakeshava Temple.'

The Naaduvaazhi's words put a smile on Devabrahma's face. The doubts he housed in his mind moments ago disappeared. He had always dreamt of conducting a Mahaa Yaagam.

'Perhaps you do not know the meaning of the word scholar.' A man from the crowd shouted.

Everyone looked around for its source. A middle-aged man dressed in rich attire made his way through the crowd and climbed up the dais.

'The *Devapreethi Maha Yaagam* calls for a scholar in all the scriptures. And you suggest a man who refers to himself as Sarvagyany. One who knows all'

'That's Vidwaan Vikramaditya Meladath.' The council members knew this man.

'I have dedicated my life to the scriptures, and there is not a written word in palm leaf that I have missed.' Devabrahma was furious to have his knowledge questioned. But he remained composed.

'All the scriptures you say? How about those in the Temple of *Rudraagni*? The Rudraagi Sutras are critical to a Devapreethi Mahaa Yaagam. Are they not written words or aren't you, one who claims to know everything, adept with the sacred language it is written in?' Meledath smiled adjusting his cufflinks. The villagers had never seen this kind of attire.

One of the council members intervened. 'Devabrahma, perhaps you are not aware. This is Vidwaan Vikramaditya Meledath from Kanthapuram. He has traveled the world and seen what no man of this land has seen.'

'What is the use of having seen the world if one cannot see what is under one's own nose?'

The praises for Meledath irritated Devabrahma further.

Meledath turned around to meet Devabrahma eye to eye.

'You are like a frog in the well *Thirumeni*. Your knowledge is limited. The Devapreethi Maha Yaagam calls for a scholar, a Vidwaan at its helm. Someone like me.'

The council member whispered amongst themselves and then one stood up 'Devabrahma Thirumeni, we respect your knowledge, but this is something that affects the whole of the land. There cannot be any flaws in the *Yaagam*. We agree with Meledath. Only one with knowledge of all the scriptures can be the *Yaaga Aacharyan*.'

He was soon seconded by the other council members. Devabrahma was not used to having his knowledge questioned. But this time self-doubt took over and he heeded. Deep in his heart Devabrahma knew that he was not aware of the inscriptions at the *Temple of Rudraagni*. He walked away into the crowd hurt by the feeling that there was someone who knew more than him. The *Paavakoothu* in the background went on and the puppet master's marionettes, Vali and Sugreeva raged a battle.

'Why did *Achha* leave? Why didn't he wait for us to finish seeing the *Paavakoothu*?' Vishnu and Maya had to walk back alone. This had never happened before. And Maya was sure that there must have been something serious. '*Achan* must be at home waiting for us. Maybe something came up. As Maya and Vishnu entered the house, they saw light in Devabrahma's study. It was the place he did all his reading. And Vishnu knew that when his father was in his study, he was not to be disturbed. But out of curiosity, he peeped in to see if Devabrahma would acknowledge his presence. Vishnu had never seen his father like this.

Devabrahma sat on the floor reading through old palm leaf scriptures. He looked for something on the Rudragni Temple. The Devanar Clan was forbidden to enter the Rudragni temple without 41 days of fasting and stringent rituals. So, to the best of his knowledge, all his ancestors kept away. He looked through every scripture he had in his collection. And finally gave up. A humble life never bothered Devabrahma. Lack of wealth, he had never even thought about. But to have his knowledge questioned, this was the first time. And that didn't let him sleep.

The *Thiruvizha* had left Parashunaadu exhausted and its head priest, disturbed and agitated. With only a lamp to light the way, Devabrahma started his journey to the Temple of *Rudragni*.

The destination was about three hours from the village and Devabrahma was certain that he could study the inscriptions and return before the morning prayers at the temple. The forest got denser as the temple approached. Vines had grown over its tall walls. For a temple that housed the knowledge that left Devabrahma's intellect inadequate, the entrance was rather small. A tiny passage that one could only enter on all fours. The priest crawled through the entrance. It was a long tunnel with inscriptions in a sacred language. The tunnel was interrupted by a statue- the *Dwarapalak* of the Temple of Rudragni. The *Dwarapalak* sat with his palms cupped behind his ears. What he read next was something Devabrahma was never prepared for.

"Enter the Temple of Devaagni holding no secrets. Enter as you have entered this earth."

Devabrahma had only one secret his whole life. The *Vaithari*. The sacred verse which hid the combination of vault locks. A part of him wanted to turn around. But the smile on Meladath's face and scorn in the eyes of the temple council made him do what he had never done before.

'The frogs together followed time, The crow, however, chose otherwise. To his call will reveal the Deva his Glory. For it is he who bears the might of the Lord.'

In his heart, Devabrahma begged the Deva for forgiveness. The *Vaithari* had never been voiced before. The statue of the Dwarapalak moved away. Devabrahma crawled on and exited the tunnel. In the large atrium before him the *Rudraagni* raged above the water in a pond.

The Rudraagni was like no other flame. It burnt with a high-pitched whine that hurt the ears. The Priest stood mesmerized. Submerged in the water, he noticed a large tablet of stone with inscriptions on it. This was the knowledge that he was here for.

'Oh, seeker of The Knowledge of the Radiant Rudraani, enter this pond as a fish for no object that man made, shall touch these waters. Oh Seeker, you pledge a vow of silence till the last words have been read. A curse will fall upon your blood to come if the silence shall you, break till the end.'

The cost of the knowledge was to remain silent till Devabrahma had finished reading the stone tablet. That was something he could manage. He disrobed and entered the water. Taking a deep breath, Devabrahma dived in to read the rest of the tablet. The light of the Rudraagni lit the part of the tablet that lay submerged. It is then that Devabrahma realised the true size of the tablet. And there were two more large ones submerged in the water, not to be seen outside. There is no way that he could finish reading these in one night.

He needed more time. Through the night, Devabrahma read the tablet, coming up for air once in a while. Dawn made its way through the large stone windows of the temple.

Devabrahma got dressed and headed back. He would return again at night to read the rest.

As he rushed up the steps of the Gajakeshava temple, he noticed something different that morning. The elephants that usually greeted him at the entrance stood with their backs turned. The younger priests were preparing for the morning rituals. Without uttering a word to anyone, Devabrahma went to bathe in the temple pond. As Devabrahma entered

the sanctum, he noticed a silence like no other day. The birds did not sing
that morning. The magpie and tailorbirds had all disappeared. As he looked
around, the lamps in the sanctum doused one after another. All the years
he spent as a priest, there was never a morning like this. He lit the lamps
with tears in his eyes. The other priests took notice of the unusual
occurrences.

Devabrahma shut himself in the temple granary for the rest of the day
and at night, went back to the Temple of Rudraagni. He spent the night
reading the tablets and, in the morning, headed back to his temple.

A large crowd had gathered at the temple that morning. On seeing
the priest, they made way for him. Devabrahma heard them whisper.
One of the junior priests ran to him. 'Thirumeni, the fish, the fish in the

temple pond are all dead. And Veerabadra…' saying this the young priest fell to his knees crying. Devabrahma ran to the mango tree where the elephant Veerabadra usually spent his time. The mighty Veerabadra was on the ground. Vishnu sat beside him crying, hugging the large animal. Devabrahma sat holding his head. Confusion clouded his thoughts. All this was too much to bear. The Naaduvaazi entered along with the Temple Council.

'What has come upon this temple?'

The council members soon summoned the astrologer who rushed to the temple. The astrologer lit his lamps and placed a board before him. With white powder, he marked the board with symbols and columns. A bunch of small seashells were placed in the center. He prayed and divided the shells into two groups. He then placed shells into the boxes he had drawn.

'The Deva does not smile anymore. A great dark cloud looms over the Gajakeshava Temple. One that will take over the whole of the land. The glory of the temple has diminished.'

The crowd was worried.

'Open the vaults. That's the glory of the temple. We need to see if the gold has been robbed.' The council member shouted. Devabrahma stood and walked to the gathering. The vault could not be opened on just any day. There were rituals that had to be performed. He had to say this to the crowd. But just as he began to talk, he was reminded of the vow of silence he had taken. Devabrahma stepped back.

'Thirumeni, open the vault at once.'

The demands from the council members were firm and the crowd turned towards the priest. Devabrama gestured that he could not. 'Why does he not speak?'

The council members went to Devabrahma and nudged him towards the vaults. And the crowd followed. As he unwillingly walked up the steps to the cave, Devabrahma tripped and fell a few times. The crowd that followed him was surprised by his silence. Behind them the junior priests, guided Sudeendra, the bearer of the Deva's ceremonial effigy. Reaching the great door of the vault, Devabrahma felt the keys tied to the robe on his shoulder. He inserted the keys adorned with the symbol of the frogs and turned them. Then he inserted the key with the symbol of the crow and turned it in the opposite direction. Devabrahma then brought forth Sudeendra who trumpeted aloud.

The great door of the vault rumbled. There were loud sounds of the deadbolts unlock. The door made way for a magnificent vault. Magnificent, but to everyone's horror, empty. The crowd went silent.

'Where? How? Who?' whispers were heard from different sides.

'The priest is the only one who can open the vault.'

A voice shouted out. And soon, every other voice concurred. Devabrahma stepped back. In his years as the head priest, he had only looked towards the gold with devotion. Never had he yearned to possess even the smallest bit of it. The acquisition was more than he could handle.

'Tell us priest, where is the gold?'

The council members took it upon themselves to question Devabrahma. They pushed forward in anger. All Devabrahma could do was plead with his hands.

'Why does he not speak? There must be something he is hiding.' The crowd noticed incantations appear on Devabrahma's body. The same that they had seen on Kethaki.

'Witchcraft!' They shouted. The mob lost its patience and attacked Devabrahma. They punched and kicked him. The priest cried helplessly. But he could not die. He could not die a thief and the only way to do that was to somehow try and prove his innocence. He had to escape from the crowd. In between the blows that fell on him, Devabrahma managed to stand up. He reached for his staff that held the hanging lamp and hurled it aimlessly in the air to distance the crowd from him.

The lamp hit a couple of people on the head. Something Devabrahma had never intended to do. But he had to keep on. Hurling the staff over and over again, Devabrahma exited the cave and ran down the steps of the temple followed by the mob. All they wanted to do now was to kill him. To block his pursuers, Devabrahma set fire to a few carts that carried hay. In his mind, he was surprised with everything he did.

Aggression had never been one of his traits. The fire stopped the crowd and Devabrahma had the time to get away and hide.

At a distance, the Naaduvaazi and Subran watched as the villagers scrambled to put out the fire.

'Parashunaadu would need a new priest now!'

A familiar voice from behind. The Naaduvaazi turned around to see Kethaki. The sorcerer had a smile which indicated that he knew everything.

'Leave Kethaki, we cannot be seen together.'

'Oh, that can be fixed.' With his toe, Ketaki drew a circle on the ground.

'Step into this *Valayam* Naaduvaazi. In here, no one can see or hear me.'

The Naaduvazhi stepped in.

'A plan well executed, Naaduvaazi. But before you celebrate victory, you have a fee to pay.'

'Only one man in Parashunaadu could have hatched a plan like that. We just executed it. What do you want, Kethaki?'

'A handful of gold from your loot. Have Subran bring it across.' 'Why not money? Why the gold? I can pay you with money' 'Let's just say there is something in that gold that is not in your money.'

Having said that, Kethaki left. Subran stood watching his master speak to himself.

It was late in the evening by the time the fire was put out. Arson was added to the list of Devabrahma's crimes. When the villagers went home, the priest came out from his hiding place. He had to find a way to convince the people. And the only way to do it was to somehow speak to the one person who could convince the people. An old friend. The Naaduvaazi.

Devabrahma ripped a piece of cloth from his shawl and wrote a message explaining everything that had happened. If he could get this across to the Naaduvaazi, everything could be set right. As Devabrahma reached the mansion, he saw the Naaduvaazi sit by a fire. He quickened his pace, but after a couple of steps, slowed down. The Naaduvaazi flipped a coin and even from a distance, Devabrahma could see the insignia of the Deva on it. Devabrahma hid by the bushes.

'Subra, you will have enough for a lifetime. Cunning old Subra, stealthy as a cat! You did your part well. The ear that heard the priest's greatest secret was yours. And the hands that stole the keys as he was in the pond. Subra, cunning old Subra.'

'When you catch a man by his weakness, anything is possible. The priest, his pride. Meledath, his dream to be the Head Priest of the Gajakeshava Temple and the council members, they always envied the respect that Devabrahma received from the people. We played each of them well Subra!'

Devabrahma wanted the Naaduvaazhi's blood. Armed with his staff in hand, he charged towards the Naaduvaazi who was caught off guard. Subran reached out for a branch and swung it hitting Devabrahma on his head. He fell to the ground and Subran pinned him down with his knee. Devabrahma tried to push himself back up, but the Naaduvaazhi stepped on his palms driving his fingers down into the ground.

'You think you can come into my house and attack me, you puny man? I take it you now know everything. The cost of some knowledge, Priest, can be your life itself.'

The Naaduvaazi grabbed his dagger.

Devabrahma was not a well-built man nor a match for the might of Subran. But the rage made him stand. Subran was thrown to the ground. Devabrahma picked up his staff and hit Subran on his chest. The Naaduvaazi was next. Hearing the commotion, Daathi and the workers ran out of the house.

'Vishnu's Achaaa!' Daathi cried at the sight.

Devabrahma froze seeing Daathi. He could not kill the Naaduvaazi now. The priest turned and ran. The workers chased him and after a distance, gave up. The maids took Daathi back into the house as she cried.

'I know where he is headed. If he completes reading the tablets at The Temple of Rudraagni, his vow of silence will be broken. He may then try to convince the people. There are things we need to do Subran.'

Devabrahma hid inside the trunk of a large tree till the pain subsided. If the villagers got hold of him, there would be no trial. Just death. He had to see Maya and Vishnu. The villagers would be guarding his house. They hated him more than anything else. He had to take a chance.

From a distance, Devabrahma saw lit torches around his house. The villagers stood guard along with the Naaduvaazhi's men. There was no way he could reach the house without being caught. His distraction, he saw in the cattle sheds of the houses nearby. After letting the animals go lose, Devabrahma set fire to the sheds. Fire had been his greatest ally that day.

As expected, the guards ran to the fire to try and douse it. Amidst the chaos, Devabrahma limped into his house. On seeing him Maya wept covering her mouth. The godly aura that she usually saw around her husband was replaced by blood and dirt. Maya turned her face away. She could not bear to see him like this. Vishnu cried and hugged his father.

Devabrahma grabbed their hands and pulled them out of the house. He wanted to get out before anyone noticed. Someone had. Subran was the only one who didn't fall for the same trick twice. Seeing the fire, he was quite sure the priest was behind it. So, he decided to hide by the house. As Devabrahma lead his family out, Subran pushed the door open and hit the priest right across the face. Devabrahma held onto his wife and child. His newfound range filled his veins, and he drove the pointed end of his lamp staff into Subran's left arm. He had aimed for the heart, but Subran was too fast for him. Devabrahma pulled his staff out as Subran sat on the ground howling with pain. There was blood all over.

The family ran out and Devabrahma pushed Maya and Vishnu into the bullock cart. All this, without a word being uttered from his mouth. Devabrahma rode the cart far from home, and when he felt that they were safe, got down from the cart and walked alongside.

The forest path was lit only by the light of the lamp that Devabrahma carried. Vishnu had gone off to sleep and every time Maya dozed off, the thoughts from that day woke her up. She could not understand her husband's silence. And could not ask. As Devabrahma walked the bollocks up the forest path, he slowly recalled the day's events. He had never hurt a man in his life. Never laid a hand, but today, he had hurt several. He could not understand how. Probably, after he had finished reading the tablets of The Temple of Rudraagni, he could try convincing his wife and son. No father wanted his son to think of him as a thief. And hopefully, he could take his family to another land and lead the life of a peasant.

The path to the temple felt longer than it usually did. Mostly because he never had to take every step with caution and fear.

A few furlongs from the temple, torches of fire suddenly sprang up from the fields around them. The Naaduvaazi stood in front along with the entire village. Subran had managed to dress his wound and he was there with all intentions to kill the priest.

Devabrahma turned the cart around and slapped the bullock on its hind. The animal drove through the crowd. Vishnu and Maya were startled, and they grabbed onto the frame of the cart. The villagers hurled stones at Devabrahma as he attempted to run. Many of the stones hit him. Vishnu shouted to his father asking him to climb up the cart. The priest tried to pick up pace. The thorns and sticks growing thick around them ripped through his flesh. Nothing stopped him. And finally, Devabrahma managed to touch the cart with the tips of his fingers. Maya and Vishnu pulled him up into the cart and he scrambled to find a way to get to the animal that were now in a frenzy.

Devabrahma suddenly felt the world around him get warmer. He looked up to see the thatch of the cart burning. The mob had hurled all sorts of things at him. But this is something he could not outrun. The animal ran through a field setting fire to everything around the cart and finally, came to a halt. The crowd looked on as the field burned and in the middle of it, the frame of a cart. Noone tried to put out the fire. The Deva had delivered his justice that night.

After fire cooks through the flesh, it touches the bone and slows down. Great beasts tossed Devabrahma's burning body. Tossed it around to keep the fire going. Tossed it around to drive more rage into the burning fire. He opened his eyes. A part of his eyelids had melted but he could see the sky move on top of him. Something had grabbed him by the right ankle and he was being pulled along the ground. Sharp stones poked into his back. The keys to the vault had become red hot in the fire. They had burnt through his chest. But he was too weak to shout.

Devabrahma looked around to see the charred remains of a field and the cart. He didn't try to look into the cart. With the little energy he had, he strained his neck to look at the person who was dragging him without mercy.

'Time, Priest has a way with mortals. It left you to live while everything around you burned to the ashes. Everyone.'

Devabrahma cried. For the first time in several days, he heard his own voice. The vow of silence was broken. He had no reason to keep it now. The pain was greater on the inside than on the outside. Maya and Vishnu were no more. Lost in the fire. Lost to the fire. Lost, because of the people of Parashunaadu.

'Pray tell, Priest, what is it that you feel inside of you? What is it that you want? There must be something you want inside of you now?''

'Death. I want death. Kill me Kethaki!'

'And what about the men who did this to you?'

In between the pain of burning flesh, anger made its way into Devabrahma's mind. The thought of everything his wife and son had gone through drove him mad.'

'Death for them Kethaki.'

'Just what I wanted to hear. And that, Priest, Kethaki can help you with.'

Devabrahma went unconscious again. The storm of thoughts in his mind left him with little energy.

'Karshanya, today we make a deal with the Fiends of the Median. Corruptible beasts who guard the gates of *Shunyalokha*, the world between afterlife and ours'

Ketaki, with the sharpened animal bone etched markings into Devabrahma's burnt body. White ropes were tied around his limbs and body. The ropes were then tied to wooden posts that kept the body suspended. Karshanya supported the body till his father was done securing the ropes. And then, let it go. The weight of his body caused the ropes to tighten, and with the unbearable pain, Devabrahma opened his eyes. Above him, he saw the mouth of a well. Kethaki's had dug a well in the middle of his Manthrashala to perform a ritual that none of his ancestors had attempted before. Devabrahma could not understand if he was dead or alive. And then remembered being dragged across the burnt field by Kethaki.

'Where are we?' He felt the ropes tighten around him as he tried to shift his body.

'What are you doing to me?'

'Helping you have your revenge.' Kethaki continued with his tattooing.

Every memory was delayed for Devabrahma. The death of his wife and son, everything head had gone through came rushing back.

'I will fix you up, Priest. I will give you the power to settle scores with this village. What can you give me in return?' 'Anything for revenge.' He saw the faces of the Naaduvaazi and the villagers before him. Each and every one of them individually. He wanted to burn everyone down. He wanted to burn everything.

'Absolute submission. All I want is absolute submission.'

'You can do whatever you want with me Kethaki. I want your magic in return.'

'And you shall have it. Karshanya will place a knife in your right hand, all you have to do is cut the thing in front of you.' Karshanya tucked a knife into Devabrahma's hands. He then held out something Devabrahma could not see. He tried to raise his head but it was held back by the ropes. He grabbed the knife and jabbed it into the thing in front. Something warm sprayed on his hands.

'Today, Priest, I am going to do a bit of a trade. Another soul, for yours. The *Fiends of the Median* will be happy with this one. It is the blood of your enemy. The blood you just spilt.'

Devabrahma's eyes followed Kethaki's voice as he got up and moved to the left. On his side was a large platform made with wood and rope. Devabrahma watched as Kethaki hoisted a girl's body onto the platform. Her wrist was cut and blood was rushing out. Devabrahma strained to look at the girl's face. And from within her wavy locks, he recognised the face of Daathi. Devabrahma shouted and pleaded. He tried to set himself free, but the ropes held him back.

Her still body lay on the white ropes above Devabrahma. He cried louder. The blood from Daathi's hand made its way to the white rope and dyed the entire length red. Soon, Devabrahma could smell the blood of the child he loved like his own. He cried out loud. Karshanya dabbed clay on his body. His limbs, his torso and finally into his mouth and nostrils. He left the hands and ears uncovered. Devabrahma could feel the cold clay solidify around him.

Kethaki kneeled in front of Devabrhama's ears. He held out a handful of gold coins from the temple vault. He threw the coins up into the air and caught it.

'Do you recognize this sound, Priest? This is the sound of your honesty. The sound of the gold you were accused of stealing.'

He then held out the keys to the vault.

'The secret you protected will make you what you are to be.'

Kethaki melted the coins with the keys and forged it into a pair of long golden fangs, claws and spikes for Devabrahma's Methiadi.

The fangs were placed on the clay that covered Devabrahma's mouth. Karshanya held the *Methiadi* to Devabrahma's feet and Kethaki hammered the spikes - Half into the wood of the methiadi and the rest into Devabrahma's feet. The claws were driven into each of his fingers. Devabrahma wailed in his mind. The soundless cries split his head. His nerves trembled.

'Pain is the cost of causing pain, Priest.'

Kethaki pulled out a strand of hair from his head along with the metal strips. He rolled the hair up into a ball around a branch. From the altar that held pure *Rudraagni*, he lit a flame and carried it to Devabrahma who was now a man-shaped clay figure. Chanting a few spells, Kethaki set fire to clay, and it burned with vigor. The ends of the ropes were tied to two small wooden poles. Kethaki sat by the poles and put on the **Hasthapa**. A gauntlet with inscriptions on it. He then wrapped the rope around his fingers. He began to make symbols with his fingers stretching the rope in between.

'This Karshanya, is the *Yoktra*. It will help me steer the souls. The *Yoktra* is to control. And the *Hasthapa*, is the right to the *Yoktra*. Some day, this will be yours. So learn it well. Tonight, with the pure Rudraagni, I will create an abomination that we can play with. An abomination with which we can remind this land of the magical prowess of the Thamoprabhu Clan. Tonight Karshanya, a man will become an animal and me, Irulnaadha Kethaki, a God.'

As Kethaki made symbols with his hands, the fire raged before him. The fangs turned red in the fire and began caving through the hard clay till it reached flesh.

Devabrahma could not scream. The clay shoved into his mouth didn't let him. As the flames caught on, demons appeared within them engulfing everything in it. Kethaki sat chanting. The night above Kethaki's Manthrashala was not dark anymore. It was lit by the flames from Kethaki's barter with the *Fiends of the Median.*

The birds and insects around the Manthrashaala didn't make it through the night. The smog that smelled of flesh, revenge and evil suffocated each and every one of them.

As the smoke cleared the well, Kethaki got up from the Yoktra. The platform that held Daathi had burnt down. The clay around Devabrahma was baked to the hardness of stone. Smoke rose from it.

'Break away the clay Karshanya.'

As Karshanya chiseled away the clay, a human figure started to appear inside it. He sped up to unveil what his father had created. And to his surprise, he saw the priest without a scratch on his body. Karshanya was expecting something, but this was just the same puny priest.

'Father, you have cured him of all his wounds. How is this an abomination?'

'Your questions will be answered, son.' Kethaki shuts his eyes.

'Arrogant of his knowledge, he was. But no one thought he could be a thief.'

'The meagre earnings of a priest must have driven him to this. The poor woman and child had to pay the price for it.'

The Naaduvaazi broke up the discussion between the council members.

'Let's lay this topic to rest and continue with the ceremony to appoint Meledath as a head priest. The Yagam has to be carried out to appease the Gods. It is more important than anything else now.'

The village had gathered to watch the rituals. Meledath entered, covered in priestly attire. A large metal tank was constructed for the ceremony. The tank was covered with sacred symbols. A long wooden platform had been erected just above the tank. Here, several priests sat chanting. Meledath sat amongst the priests and prayed to the fire at the altar. He then joined in making offerings to the various gods. The ceremony went on for several hours.

In the end, Meledath was to take a dip in the ceremonial metal tank. The priests guided him into the tank. The tank had four metal steps. With his hands folded in prayer, Meledath slowly descended into the water till he was completely submerged. The priests on the platform prayed and threw flowers into the water. The man who would climb out of the tank would be the next Head Priest of Gajakeshava Temple.

'Man, is never content with the place he holds.'

Meledath was startled by the voice and he opened his eyes. In front of him, he saw a blurred figure seated. The figure shifted with the ripples of the water and Meledath strained to make sense of the shape.

On the surface, the ceremonies continued with the beating of drums and the sounds of conch shells. The priests and the people eagerly waited for Meledath to climb out of the tank. Several moments later, the sounds slowly subsided, and the priests began looking at each other. An atmosphere of music and pomp suddenly became silent. 'Someone, get in.' A voice stammered from the crowd. One of the younger priests jumped into the water. Moments later he sprang out and called on his companions. As the priests dived into the water, they saw the cold dead body of Meledath with his feet hammered onto the floor of the tank.

'The *Dvipanta*, when it rocks can teleport the Jendhu. He will have access to the new world as long as the *Dvipanta* swings.' Karshanya sat listening to his father. The Dvipanta was a large metal *Yantr* with a parabolic base. It was covered with spikes and incantations in *Thamolipi*, a language used by Kethaki in his dark arts.

'The *Jendhu* is stronger than you think and when you are on the Yoktra, you should focus without any distractions. And whatever happens, your toes are never to touch the earth when you are in control of the ropes of the Yoktra. You can lose control of the *Jendhu*.'

Devabrahma sat on a pedestal unconscious entangled in the red rope stained with the blood of Daathi.

'It's time for the priest to realize what he has become and what he is capable of doing.'

Kethaki had his fingers looped in the ropes of the Yoktra. He made a *Mudra* with his hands and tugged on the rope. Red dust formed around the priest. Demons formed from the dust screeched and circumvented him. The fangs pierced out of his face and the claws out of his fingers. Devabrahma grew in size and the beast growled in pain. '*Parinathi*, the transformation. 'The *Jendhu*'. Kethaki looked at his creation and smiled in pride. The abomination growled and tugged on the ropes that held him.

'Kethaki, what have you made of me?'

'Everything you never were, *Jendhu*. How does vengeance feel? Did Meledath scream?'

'More, I want more. *Parashunaadu* will bleed.'

The abomination sat on thin air with one leg folded over his lap and one toe touching the ground. His right arm rested on the lamp staff.

'You will have your revenge, *Jendhu.* In return for absolute submission to me. Your master.'

'Anything for revenge. Just set me free again.'

'When the time is right.' Saying that, Kethaki made another *Mudra* with his hands and slacked the ropes. The abomination transformed back to its human form and fell to the ground.

'Why does he have to go back into the form of the Priest, father. Why can't we keep him as the beast.'

'Karshanya, what you see before you is an undead form of Devabrahma. His soul was returned to me for the price of the child's. A soul stained by the blood of the same child. The Inferno of pure Rudragni gave him the powers he has now. To keep him in control, I have given the Jendhu a flaw. A flaw that lets me control him. The Jendhu' s weakness is the priest's conscience that lies dormant in him. His last human element.'

Kethaki had triumphed. He stood proud in front of Karshanya.

"Can the doors of your *Nilavara* hold the sheen of your gold...Naaduvaazi?"

He could smell the gold. And what if others could? As he slept the Naaduvaazhi's eyebrows began to twitch. Long golden nails ran through the Naaduvaazhi's hair.

"Sleep well Naaduvaazi just as your gold".

The Naaduvaazhi's head rested comfortably on the lap of an abomination he could have never seen outside of a dream.

Startled, the sleeping man jumped up. The creature he rested his head on, was gone. The Naaduvaazi ran out of his chamber into the hall. As he opened his door, he saw his servants walk about flaunting the gold he thought was hidden away. They paid him no heed. Some smiled at him.

'You sons of dogs...the audacity to lay your filthy eyes on my gold'. Grinding his teeth, not bothering to dress himself, the Naaduvaazi ran into the courtyard and grabbed a tree bark from the heap of firewood that was arranged to prepare his bath. The servants walked around him holding the gold close to their bare chest.

'Drop my gold you animals'.

The Naaduvaazhi swung the firewood and crushed the skull of a servant who approached him. He looked around to see others walk past, not alarmed by the blood or the action. 'Dogs. All of you'.

The Naaduvaazi scrambled around the courtyard swinging at the servants he could see. Breaking bones, killing them all till there was no one else to kill.

'You dogs think you can get away with my gold'.

A battered body drenched in blood looked up at the Naaduvaazi from where he lay. Not knowing what he had just been slaughtered for.

'Subra…get here at once…burn these dogs. These thieving sons of dogs'

The Naaduvaazi pushed himself up and slipped on the floor drenched with the blood of men who served him all his life. His *Mundu*, otherwise bright as the sky, trailed behind him. He walked to the next room still holding the weapon he had acquired.

'Subra…'

'No! not you too'

Subra sat squatting. Eating gold from a plate. Pushing gold down his throat. He looked up at the Naaduvaazi and continued to eat. This time, his master's presence meant nothing.

'Filthy conniving wretch…'.

A jolt ran up the Naaduvaazhi's arms as wood crushed through Subra's skull and met the wall behind. The mass of the henchman twitched on the ground longer than the servants. They were easier to kill. The frail men they were.

'My gold…he eats my gold'

Pieces of Subra scattered all around. Interrupted between his regular afternoon meal.

The Naaduvaazi ran to the *Nilavara* and bolted the door from the inside. The trunks of gold around him shone like the day he had acquired them. He looked around and made sure that all the doors and windows were shut.

'Let's see who gets to my gold now'.

He sat on one of the trunks. The firewood he decided to keep close.

'The sheen of gold can never be contained Naaduvaazi' 'Who is that?…show yourself servant'. He grabbed his club. 'Be one with your gold, Naaduvaazi'

The Naaduvaaazi looked around. The gold in the trunks began to melt. Melt into flowing liquid form, still shining like in its previous life. From all around him, the melted gold flowed towards him. Like they were being attracted towards him. He was entranced by the sheen of flowing liquid gold. But the trance was broken when the metal burnt through the skin on his toes to the flesh and then the bone behind it. The gold he loved ate him alive, cooking every inch of his body. The flowing hot gold flooded the room. All around the Naaduvaazi who could smell the gold mixed with the smell of his charred bones. Pain like this can never be described. All he could do was scream. Louder and louder as the metal inched its way up. Burning everything it was engulfing.

Workers on the field washed themselves in a stream nearby and headed to collect the day's wages from the Naaduvaazi as they always did at the end of every workday. The house was not its active self. No servants or the Naaduvaazi shouting orders at them. Today it was silent. Today, it had witnessed the slaughter of servants who went about their daily duties and disembowelment of a henchman who sat down to eat a meal. The workers looked about in shock, making their way through the hall of bodies. They surveyed for the Naaduvaazhi opening all doors till they came across one that was bolted shut. Not hearing a response to their calls, they broke down the door to find a charred body in the middle of the room. A room that held the treasure of Deva. All intact. Shining in large wooden trunks.

The people realized that they had convicted an innocent man. But it was not sympathy they felt now. It was a deep fear. The death of Vikramaditya Meledath and the Naaduvaazi were terrifying. Soon after, the bodies of three members of the temple council were found. They had battered each other to death. Fear spread through the village. Parashunaadu was dealing with an ungodly entity.

'Jendhu.'

'Now you know what you are capable of. The vengeance of the priest is finally over'

'I want more' snarled Brahma.

'The lost glory of the Thamoprabhu clan! With you I can take that all back. '

'You command me? You have seen what I can do. Eyes down before me Kethaki.'

Brahma stretched the ropes of the Yoktra that he had been entangled in. Kethaki could see the pupil of his eyes in the shine of Brahma's fangs. Kethaki pulled on one of the ropes with his little finger. Brahma became motionless again. Down on his knees. The man that made the beast had also made means of containing it. The Yoktra. Brahma was bound to it like an animal to his cart and the master.

'An animal. Just a mere animal. Brahma'.

And I have a purpose for your Brahma. Like all creatures made on earth, you bear a purpose as well.

'Learn to accept me as your lord. And I will show you the limitations of your previous birth. The one you wasted worshiping a God who had the power of a dormant pillar.'

Kethaki sat cross legged at his end of the Yoktra. He ran the ropes across his fingers. Made sacred signs with the rope. The ropes were never strong enough to hold Brahma. But the magic in them and the debt of the blood of a child that dried up along the rope, could contain even stronger beasts. Slowly, the fangs disappeared. The beast turned into the priest. The strong monstrous body strung to the Yoktra fell to the ground. Frail as the priest once was.

'What is happening Kethaki?' The priest asked in a feeble voice. His eyes looked around Kethaki's *Manthrashaala*. Looking for answers, not aware of the hours that had passed.

'Man created a God, Priest. Go back to sleep. I'll wake you up when I need you'.

Kethaki chanted a spell and left.

Fear catches on faster than fire. And fear, like fire, grows stronger. The village had killed an innocent priest and his family, and they knew that everything that followed was a repercussion of the events tainted with supernatural influence. Fear grows when things that happen lack explanation. And with fear, mistrust and hostility made themselves felt. The smell of ash replaced the floral atmosphere of Parashunaadu. Children never came out to play. Festivals and celebrations were called off. And when they weren't, a natural calamity ensured that they never happened.

Lakes ran dry and the seasonal rains that normally filled the lakes caused floods that toppled houses. The villagers didn't know what to pray for. Disease was rampant. And death was the only solace left in nature. Parashunaadu had to finally take refuge under the locks of Kethaki. Under the magic that they had forgotten.

'Pray to a force that is concerned enough to answer. Pray through Kethaki and we can put your gods to shame'.

And Kethaki did deliver. The enemies of those who worshiped Ketaki's gods were vanquished and wishes fulfilled. Every one of them. Without delay or procrastination of nature. For a simple cost of undying devotion to the new force. The force that never hesitated to grant wishes. No one knew what this force was or where it came from. All that they knew that the force protected them from the curse of the priest.

The people who despised the Thamoprabhu Clan, soon became followers. At first it was the villagers who came for help. And then kings of provinces. Kethaki was paid well, and he gave them what they wanted. But it was more than wealth for Kethaki. His triumph was in submission.

But then, Kethaki nor the beast never took sides. The magic was for everyone. The *Jendhu* and Kethaki instigated battles and watched everything around burn. The Jendhu was completely under Kethaki's command and magic. He controlled him with the one weakness that he had created him with. The priest within. But with the taste of blood and victory, the abomination began to feel his power. With every soul that the Jendhu consumed, the priest in him died a little more. And in time, Kethaki struggled to control him with the Yoktra, the harness.

The King of Parashunaadu was secretly a patron. He paid for the magic to be undefeated in war. Cheraramapuram was in constant battle with Parshunaadu. The French East India company looked at this battle with great interest. They wanted authority over Parashunaadu to gain access to the mountains of Parashunaadu. With control over the mountains, they could control the water. And when you control water, you control the world. The French had their arms around both shoulders. And their knives. They fed Cheraramapuram with everything it took to keep the war going and at the same time sent envoys to Parashunaadu. But guns were nothing against Kethaki's magic. And nobody knew that. Charles Dieudonne Aubert took over as General de Brigade of the French East India Company. And he was to bring Parashunaadu under his control by all means possible.

Destiny, follows no rules of engagement. Karshanya, Kethaki's only son was a lad of short temper. After a brawl with a few outsiders, he decided to get back at them with the beast. Karshanya took hold of the Yoktra to command the beast in the absence of his father, the imbecile he was. The boy's magic was not strong enough to control the beast. The Jendhu ripped Karshanya into shreds before disappearing from Kethaki's

Manthrashaala. When Kethaki cried, every remaining blade of grass in Parashunaadu burnt to ashes. He swore to put an end to the abomination he had created.

The *Rudirachakra,* a magical device that Kethaki had forged, pointed the way to the beast at the cost of a drop of blood. Kethaki traveled without stopping for four days and four nights. And as he moved, drew up plans to destroy the beast. On the fifth day, the Rudirachakra pointed to the market. As Kethaki entered, he saw men fight mercilessly. The ground was covered in blood. And in between all of it, visible only to Kethaki, sat the Jendhu enjoying the fight he had created. The Jendhu had grown to enjoy bloodshed.

Kethaki hurled the reigns of the Yoktra at the Jendhu. He burst into the wind and appeared in another place. The *Jendhu* smiled, mocking Kethaki. He hurled the reins again and again, but the Jendhu had learned how to get away. Stronger than he was ever before. The men around continued to fight each other. Mere mortals could never see the Jendhu with their disgusting eyes. The Jendhu laughed at Kethaki as he shifted effortlessly from place to place through the air.

But Kethaki had the one thing that could bring him under his feet. From his satchel, he pulled out an earthen pot filled with the ashes of the priest's son and wife. And shouting out to him, hurled it onto the ground covered with blood. Kethaki looked into the Jendhu's eyes and watched the fire in it disappear. Before the pot touched the ground, a hand caught it. The priest, inside the Jendhu. That, Kethaki still had control over. The priest was not strong enough for the reins that dragged him. As he was dragged back to the *Manthrashaala*, the beast would appear and shout insults at the priest within him. Cursing him for the weakness that Kethaki had put in.

The full moon night that followed. Kethaki prepared his *Manthrashaala* for the last ritual he would perform. The beast was locked in a golden receptacle made to the size of the priest in a meditating posture. The receptacle would be fired in pure *Devaagni* and with the destruction of his creation, Kethaki would take his own life. Kethaki had preserved the Eternal *Devaagni*, once lit by Devabrahma in the Gajakeshava temple. The *Devaagni*, was now the only force on earth that could end the beast. Kethaki doubted if the beast had grown beyond conventional rules of his craft. But he had to go through with the ritual. Kethaki was tired and distraught. And more than physical fatigue the thought of his only son in shreds broke him down further. This was the last of the eternal flame there was. Preserved by the Devanaar clan since the day they were entrusted with it by the saints who mastered it. And with Devabrahma being the last of the clan, it would die with the ritual

Red ropes of the Yoktra ran over the receptacle and at the other end, Kethaki bound his entire body. Kethaki set fire to the logs below the receptacle. Each log bore magical symbols on it. As the fire started to catch on, the receptacle began to rise in the air. With the ropes of the Yoktra between his fingers, Kethaki made symbols in the air. Kethaki had been prepared to face every celestial hindrance between the ritual. The Fiends of the Median would try to stop the ritual and Kethaki had the magic to control everything. Everything but one. The disruption of man.

At the very time, the Manthrashaala was raided by French soldiers commanded by General Charles. Kethaki tried to resist. He even managed to injure a few soldiers but he was too weak to fight on with magic, muscle or heart. The chaos left Kethaki severely injured. His possessions, including the receptacle, were confiscated and moved to the military camp. The white man fell for the sheen of the gold. Charles watched on as his men made shambles of the Manthrashaala. Kethaki repeatedly warned Charles and his men but no one listened.

The Legion celebrated for a night. In between the raid, the men had also pocketed gold and money. But when one possesses something so evil, there are bound to be effects. Charles received orders the next day to transport all the confiscated goods to Oberalp, the military base in Switzerland

and he duly loaded everything on the first ship off the coast.

The nights that followed, Charles began to see the outcomes of his action. Strange incantations appeared all over his body and he often dreamt of being suspended from a rope. Strange voices drove him insane and he began to doubt if Kethaki was the cause. He spoke to no one. He feared that if his men or the command heard of his experience, they would brand him as a mad man. And that could result in deportation and dismissal from the army.

Kethaki's Manthrashaala was not a place where any man walked into, alone. Not at night, not even in the day. Charles didn't have a choice.

'You have come for answers, Pardesi?' Kethaki felt Charlse's presence from the mat he was lying on. His wounds were infected, and his body was weakened by the fever.

'I need explanations for whatever has been happening.'

Charles was not going to display his vulnerability to Kethaki. He shrouded his confused and broken self with the authoritative tone his post had instilled in him.

'Pride, Pardesi, in the presence of Irulnaadha Kethaki, would have normally cost you your life. But I have no worse suffering to bestow upon you than the one you are to experience.'

Kethaki slowly crept out of his mat and grabbed a handful of powder from an earthen pot. Whispering a spell, he threw the powder into a large metal vessel with water. The powder floated on the water and slowly began to move around to form an image. Charles strained his eyes and slowly the image became clearer. He saw the familiar face of his wife Amelia on a rocking chair peacefully singing to his newborn son. The child's hair glowed in the morning window light. But there was something long and sharp that ran slyly through the baby's hair. The powder moved on the water to reveal another part of the image and there, he saw the most frightening sight he had ever witnessed. A large beast that stood like a man with golden fangs ran his large golden claws through the hair of his child from behind as his wife sat peacefully singing a lullaby on the chair.

'Yajamanasya Swagathamasthi' It said looking towards Charles.

The powder mixed into the water, and with it, the image disappeared. Charles lost his breath and fell to his knees.

'That Pardesi, is the punishment for your insolence.' 'What, who is that?' Charles cried.

'That is what the receptacle you stole from me contained. A beast capable of doing more than what your entire army can. A beast that is no longer bound by my magic. The receptacle, once taken across the sea, can no longer contain the *Jendhu*. You are the reason he is free now. And you are his new *Yajamanan* and lord. A lord who has to feed and appease him. For without my magic, the *Jendhu* is no longer submissive. In time, the Jendhu will amass godly strength and you have to witness it all.' Frail and wounded, Kethaki managed to laugh out loud.

Chapter 5
Closer

Liam licked his fingers off the sauce from the sandwich he had just eaten. Nathan and the rookie looked at each other. They didn't know how the story they had just heard could have had any bearing on what happened in Schwarzenberg.

'These are the stories I heard in the castle where I was held captive. The narrator, I do not know. All I heard was his voice. I don't know how I managed to get out. One day, I heard nothing around me. I ran and with luck, made it out of the castle.'

'Do you remember anything else from the castle? Any voices that you can recognize?'

'No, nothing at all.'

'Maybe, you should come with us. I can't leave you here by yourself.'

The rookie helped Liam into the back seat of his car. The rookie offered to drive. Nathan was disturbed. He still had unanswered questions. He knew there was more to Liam's story. It had something to do with him.

'Did you run a search on those symbols I sent you?' 'Detective, those markings, I ran them through the database. These have come up in pictures from all over the world. Some sort of crazy cult worship. Mostly from crime scenes. Missing people, mutilated bodies, human sacrifice. But the investigations ended there. All dead ends. No one had tried to put it all together. The language is not related to anything in the database. Definitely foreign. Maybe ceremonial.'

'When I think about it now, I've seen these before. During an extraction mission. There were markings like these all over, but we didn't pay much attention to them. The site was covered with graffiti. This was many years ago. The mission that cost me my leg.' Nathan felt the rookie needed to know more.

'A high-profile individual had been kidnapped. So high profile that they even wanted to keep the rescue mission classified. My unit was called in. None of us knew who was to be rescued. The kidnappers were operating out of an old Nazi torture camp. And you know torture camps. They are so grim you can hear voices and screams from the walls.'

The corridors were booby trapped so I sent a reconnaissance drone ahead of the men. We were operating it from the command center. As the drone flew through, I picked up words in a foreign language. And between the static, I saw a figure. Back then, I thought it was some sort of interference. Thinking back, I'm quite sure it was this creature. The creature was there. We ignored everything then. I didn't pay attention to any of those things. It was then that I detected a trip wire. I tried to warn my men, but the static was so high, I couldn't get through to them. I ran out of the van but before I could get to the room, the bomb had gone off killing my men. Right before my eyes.

After the explosion, the kidnappers escaped from the side of the camp in an SUV. I was not going to let them go. I caught up with them and rammed into their vehicle. Three men broke their way through the mangled car. They had what appeared to be a child with them in blind fold. They shot at me, and I shot back. I got two of them. When the third man ran out of ammunition, I beat the daylights out of the bastard. I secured the child in my car and went back to get the man. You know what's weird rookie? The man kept smiling. And he told me something even weirder. The kidnapping was planned by the child's father for political mileage. Saying that, he pulled the pin from a grenade on his vest. All these years, I never understood what I saw there. When life took over, I began to forget. Now I know that all these events are related. The unit was disbanded after the mission. There were not a lot of us left behind.'

Visions from his past flashed through his mind. The faces of his old friends who he had fought death with.

The landscape changed around him and Nathan slept off. Thoughts still stormed inside him. When he woke up, the car was not moving. Sensing a commotion behind him, Nathan looked back outside the car where the rookie was trying to strangle Liam. Nathan ran out and hit the rookie on the head and he fell unconscious. He helped Liam into the car and tied up the rookie.

'That man just attacked me for no reason. He stopped the vehicle, dragged me out and started hitting me.'

'It's happening to him as well. Just like the trekkers.'

Nathan loaded the rookie into the boot and drove off. At Werthenstein, Nathan locked the rookie into one of the cells and asked Freston to feed him something once he was awake. Freston never tried to understand anything. Everything went above his head. Elsa Carli sat in the adjoining cell, expressionless. Nathan took her to the interrogation room. She followed him without resisting. He sat her down and gave her a cup of coffee. He pushed the record button on the camera and opened the folder that the rookie had brought along.

Nathan began to arrange the file photographs before her on the table. He hoped that one of them would jog her memory. They did much more. Elsa began to shiver and then shouted in a foreign language. Nathan stood back. That was not the reaction he was expecting. And in a split second, Elsa broke her neck with her own hands. The body fell heavily to the ground. Nathan ran to check for a pulse. Elsa Carli was dead. The captain and Freston came running in.

As the medics wrapped the body and carried it away, Nathan sat on the chair in the room. He had never seen a person do what Elsa just did. He and the captain ran through the recording over and over again. Elsa had clearly reacted to the pictures with the symbols.

Later that night, Nathan drove back to The White Crown. Burhman was eager to know what had happened. But Nathan could not put words together to explain anything. Burhman got the point. The children took the bedroom in the cabin. Burhman stretched on the long couch and Nathan sat by the chair near the fireplace with Liam on his side, scribbling in a small sketchbook. The children had taken a liking to Liam. They spent the evening looking through his books.

'You never find children like yours these days. They grow up too fast too soon. Childhood innocence fades faster than it used to.' For a blind man, Liam was sharp on observation. 'They take after their mother.' Nathan slowly fell asleep. It had started to snow outside the cabin.

The past few days made Nathan look into his past more than any time before. He was too busy with life. The answers to the present, were in the past. And that didn't even leave him alone in his dreams.

He began to think of the children's mother. The day he lost her. Actually, the day he lost her again.

A summer in 2010, Nathan was assigned to escort a key witness to a safe house in Schwarzenberg. The identity of the witness was classified. Nathan and his partner were to meet the convoy at a point 14 miles from Schwarzenberg. The instructions were clear- The witness would be in an armored truck with two escort vehicles. The GPS tracking information was sent to Nathan only at the moment he reached the rendezvous point. He followed it carefully. The convoy would not stop anywhere and Nathan would have to escort them from the front.

As Nathan looked at the moving dot on his map, it suddenly stopped. About a mile off. He waited for a few minutes. It was probably a traffic hold up. Nathan radioed the team leader to confirm. The radio was silent. Sensing something wrong Nathan drove to the location. From a distance, he heard firing. The convoy was under attack. The assailants were heavily armed, and the team was outnumbered. Nathan shot at the assailants from the cover of his car. They fired back. A bullet got his partner on the head. The convoy leader, threw Nathan an M16. Nathan opened fire at the assailants. He shot the petrol tank of their truck and took down one vehicle. Using the burning vehicles as cover, Nathan made it to the armored truck. The tires had been blown off with a mine. Several officers were shot. One of the assailants had hold of the witness who he had bagged till the shoulder. Nathan sprang up at the man and pushed him away from the witness. The assailant dropped his rifle. The men rolled, punching each other. Nathan hit the man till he was too weak to fight back. He had to now secure the witness.

As Nathan got up and ran to the witness, the assailant on the ground pulled out a handgun and shot. Nathan watched the bullet miss him by an inch and pierce the witness in the chest. As the witness fell to the ground, Nathan pulled the body behind the truck hoping the wound was not fatal. He pulled the bag off the witness's head to look for a pulse.

It was Claire.

All these years, he had never seen her. Louise had moved to another town after the Lauder incident. The wound was deep. The bullet had pierced through her heart. Nathan had changed, but she could recognize him from the eyes.

The rage inside Nathan grew and it drove him insane. He pulled out a metal pipe from the mangled pile and instantaneously smashed the assailant's head into the ground. He threw himself into the action and shot at the remaining assailants. And even after he killed them, he continued to shoot at their bodies till he ran out of rounds. He ran back. Claire could not talk. All she did was point to the truck. And then, her hand plopped to the ground. Nathan hugged the bleeding body. The only person who was kind to him and understood him, was dead.

Nathan ran to the truck and pulled open the door. In the corner, little Eva sat scared with Holly wrapped in a blanket.

'You found her, to lose her again. Didn't you?' Liam had not slept.

'Have I been talking in my sleep again?' Nathan sat up and rubbed his eyes.

'The children, you love them like your own.'

'They are all I have. Where's Burhman?'

'You keep forgetting that I am blind.'

Nathan looked around the room. Burhman was nowhere to be found. Between the sound of the night, there was something that sounded quite peculiar. And that grew louder as Nathan listened.

Chanting!

Moving the curtain aside, Nathan looked out into the night. Red mist had formed outside the cottage and swirling in the mist were red demonic faces. The chanting got louder and the mist got closer. The demons stuck their serpent tongues out. Nathan ran to the room with the children. He picked Holly up and grabbed hold of Eva's hands. Someone held Nathan by the shoulder and pushed him away.

Behind him, Burhman stood with blank eyes. Red incantations had covered his body and he moved towards Nathan and the children. Nathan kicked Burhman away, carried the children out of the room and bolted it from outside. The red mist had made its way in through the cracks in the window.

'Get Liam, Holly. There is a cellar here somewhere.'

Nathan looked around and found the cellar at the far end of the room. He smashed the lock with an axe and went in with the children and Liam. The walls of the cottage were rattling loudly. With his phone, Nathan lit the inside of the cellar. The chanting was getting louder on the outside and the cottage shook like it were in the midst of a hurricane. He set holly down and tucked in her blanket. Eva sat shivering at the end of the cellar. Nathan wasn't sure if they would make it. He looked around and grabbed an ice axe from a pile, waiting for whatever that would make it through the door.

Eva, was the only one not affected by anything. She sat with a little paper bird, curled up in her sister's lap. From the gap between the planks of the cellar door, the red mist seeped in and not before long, the mist, blustering with demons and creatures formed a circle around Nathan and the girls. Nathan hurled the axe but all it did was cut through the air. The circle got smaller and Nathan tried to cover the children with his body. He tightened his grip as he felt the cold breath of the creatures by his ears. And then, all of a sudden everything stopped moving. Everything went silent. And the red maddening mass disappeared.

The children were not harmed and Liam, thanks to his blindness, did not have to witness the horror. Nathan sat with the children for several hours and when he was sure that they were not in danger, let go. The children were asleep, bundled up on the floor. Nathan surveyed the cellar for anything usable. The light from his phone fell on a large heap on the side. These were trekking bags. Scores of them. All piled up.

Some had name tags on them. Nathan quickly took photographs of the names on the tags.

The morning light was visible through cracks in the ceiling of the cellar. Nathan had to get out. Slowly he made his way up the steps carrying Holly in one hand. He pushed the door open and climbed up. Eva helped Liam out of the cellar. As Nathan looked around the cottage, he understood that the ordeal was not over. The cottage around them had been shattered but the pieces were held up in the air. An explosion, frozen in time. As Nathan and the children looked around, the pieces slowly fell to the ground exposing the land around.

There was nothing Nathan could recognize in the new surroundings.

The cottages were gone, and the landscape was completely changed. There was no snow on the ground. Just dry red earth. And on the ground, were several heaps of mud that concealed bodies till the feet. Nathan walked on slowly with Eva clinging on to him with one hand and the other around Liam's hand. The toes on the feet started to move and seeing them Eva cried. Nathan hurried and reached the car. They got in quickly. As he drove, Nathan looked around. Werthenstein had completely changed. Wooden cottages and stone buildings were now houses with large sloping roofs. People walked past near them. People with darker skin and non-European features. None of them noticed Nathan and the car. They all said just one thing.

'We bear witness'.

Nathan did not know what that meant. Nothing made sense. Nothing ever did in this place. This was not just an illusion that Nathan saw. Eva and Holly saw it too. Overnight, they had been transported to a different land. But how could that be even possible? This had to be some sort of mind game someone was playing. In front of the car, all of a sudden, a man with fangs painted on his face jumped onto the way carrying a large grotesque figurine with beasts crawling around it. Nathan drove through the man and in a moment, everything around them burst into red dust.

Now, Nathan now saw familiar landscapes. The mind game had ended. For now.

The road out of Werthenstein was covered in snow, so there was no getting out. Nathan had to take the children to the police station. He felt safe in a place with guns. The captain was out as usual leaving the station to the mercy of Freston's inexperience. Nathan put the children to sleep in the waiting room. Eva was shaken, but Holly seemed to be calm. Uncomfortably calm.

'Liam, what is happening around us? I don't want to believe anything I saw. But I saw all that.'

'I could feel everything detective. I know what you went through.'

'I am a part of all this. I know that. I can't seem to understand it, but I know it. Maybe the explanations lie in that fort they took you to.'

All the logic in Nathan's mind had made way for confusion and doubt. He knew that the only way he could keep the children safe was to go straight to the reason behind all this before anything came to them.

'You look for a river and a large bridge that runs over it. A bridge with cobblestones.'

Liam knew what Nathan would do next.

'Freston, Liam, I leave the children in your care. Please call the captain and ask him to get here.'

Freston, was making hot chocolate for the children. In spite of this usual carelessness, Freston would at the least keep the children fed on time. Nathan was sure of that.

'Eva, I need you to take care of your sister. I'll be back soon. While you are at that, do take care of Liam and Freston. Make sure Freston does not play with fire or stick his finger up the socket.' Nathan winked at Freston.

Eva was still blank, but she understood that her father was about to do something dangerous. She hugged him and cried. 'You are in charge eva. Like you have always been. I have to make all this go away and you are the only person who can help me do that.'

Nathan had raised her to be strong and listening to him speak, she knew that this was no time for fear.

'You get back soon, detective. I'll watch the kids.' Holly knew this would make him stronger.

With the descriptions from Liam, Nathan sat at the computer to try and find the castle he spoke about. In a 100-mile radius, there was only one fort castle that stood by a river- Castle Oberalp. Eight watchtowers on the surrounding hills guarded the stronghold back in the day. This is where Nathan had to go to find an answer.

Nathan loaded all the guns he could find into the car. He marked his destination on the phone and set off. He hadn't thought anything through. All he wanted were answers. Nathan watched the spot on the map move closer to Castle Oberalp. The landscape had changed and all he could see around him were snow covered mountains. And in the distance, from between the mountains, rose strong, bold Castle Oberalp. The castle dominated the area. Its bulk spoke of times when the lords who owned it, had things to protect. And to this day, Oberalp was protecting something.

The road ended. Nathan had to climb down a small valley before he could reach the bridge that Liam had mentioned. Loading the guns into the pockets in his jacket, Nathan stepped out of the car. The jacket felt heavy. Nathan didn't know if guns could protect him from anything he was about to encounter. But as always, he felt safer with guns. The path, filled with sharp black stones, was flat with small patches of snow. As he walked on, Nathan could hear the wind blow through the mountains. But then, everything went silent. So silent, that Nathan could hear his own breath. And then, the red mist started to appear. Nathan was at the right place.

Nathan turned around and he could not see his car anymore. As he looked around him, he saw people walk in from thin air. They walked around him lifeless without taking notice of anything. 'We bear witness' is all they said. They didn't see Nathan. They saw nothing. How could they with pale white eyes? Amongst them a man holding gold coins ran around like he was running from something. 'Hide my gold' he shouted.

Nathan could not stop or turn around now. A red storm began to build up around him. And by the second, it got stronger. Incantations appeared in the storm all around him. Nathan reached for his gun, but as the storm hurled around him, his jackets and clothes disintegrated along with the weapons. He was now draped in red attire. His chest, bare but for red markings. And on his right hand a golden gauntlet had formed. That too bore incantations. The voices around him grew louder. 'We bear witness' the men and women around him said together. Nathan pushed himself through the storm. The red dust formed into faces that screeched at him. Words from a language he had never heard before. Nathan walked on till he felt cobblestones under his feet. The dust began to retreat.

Nathan saw the bridge over the river, at its end Castle Oberalp.

'*Yajamanasya Swagathamasthi*' a voice boomed from within the castle. Nathan forced himself to walk on. He looked down from the bridge into the water several feet below. Castle Oberalp was covered in moss and vines. The trees in the compound had grown into the windows and open corridors. It was clear that this place had been abandoned for years. Abandoned by men. Not by forces that Nathan could feel now. There were incantations all around the castle. Faces were carved into barks and branches of trees. Demonic faces that watched over the castle and anyone who entered.

The gates of the castle and doors were open. Whatever was inside, was waiting for Nathan. He was aware of that. He just didn't know why. Nathan entered a large empty hall. Three spiral staircases at the end of the hall lead to separate hallways. Nathan took the one in the middle. Like he knew where to go. Like something was guiding him through. As he stood in the darkness of the hallway, he could hear someone talk. Not the chanting that he had heard before. These were legible words. He walked on slowly. The voice came from a room at the end of the hallway.

'That's blood I know. Come closer, *Pardesi*.'

There was someone there. Someone too weak to move. The light from the window lit a small portion of the room. And there, Nathan saw an old man suspended within a large golden ring. The vines had grown all around the room. The man looked old. Really old.

Nathan looked up at the man. He could see the pain in his eyes. His scrawny body was tied to the ring like an insect in a web.

'Who are you?'

'Yes this is blood I know. He finally got you here. Didn't he?' 'Who? Who are you talking about? How do you know me?' Nathan's battery of questions came out unhindered.

'You know that this is where you are supposed to be *Pardesi*. You just don't know why.' The old man strained to talk. The red ropes tied to the end of his long hair pulled on every strand. And Nathan could hear the pain in the man's voice.'

'I can't seem to understand anything, old man. I should try and get you down from this contraption.'

'No, you cannot. This is my prison. I am held here by a magic you do not know. The same magic that brought you here. The same magic that I once wielded.'

'Was it you who told the painter the story of the beast? The priest that some Kethaki turned into a beast?'

'Irulnaadha Thamoprabhu Kethaki! You say my name with respect, *Pardesi*.'

'It was you? How have you been alive all these years? That's impossible.'

'The beast you spoke of has kept me on as a spectator. A witness to his growth to the place of a God. Along with the souls who walk outside this castle. The souls of the people from our land wander around him. He wants us all to bear witness to what he is about to become. The Priest had his vengeance through the *Jendhu*. Meledath, the temple council and all the villagers who threw stones at him now walk in the Field of Wanderers. They amuse the Jendhu. He has his vengeance by never letting their souls rest. The man you saw run around with gold in his hands is the Naaduvaazi. He hasn't realized the death that burnt him. Me, he kept alive to witness his ascent to Goddom.'

'For I am his creator. And in the coming days, he will be stronger than the creator's creator. The beast is no longer the toy that I had conjured once.'

'The Jendhu. Today, he is Lord to the Fiends of the Median'. 'The Fiends- Beasts so fearsome that even the Gods let them roam. Their function in the cosmos is integral to the cycle of life and death. But the function given to them by the cosmos makes them vulnerable to corruption.

And you were the last piece instrumental to his ascension.'

'Me? Why me?'

'You? You ask yourself, why you? Each of us is more than what we understand of ourselves. We are products of the past we have seen and even those we cannot. You bear on your shoulder the weight of an ancestor's deed. Your father and his father before, have paid the price. All the successors of Charles Dieudonne Aubert. The man who released the beast. The *Jendhu* that I created. When one steals the beast, he becomes the new *Yajamanan*, the owner. The beast is then his to feed. Now your's *Pardesi*. That is your only destiny. Like a cat playing with his catch, he will play with you. Break you as he has done through your life. Break you like they break a wild animal. Do you think your life has been under your control? Ever since the beast learnt of the surviving lineage, he has tried to break every one of you. Break them to the extent of hating life. Making it easier to lure you in. Making you gullible. Weak!'

'The *Pardesis* always felt they had the world under their feet. But the day Charles came running to me, I had one at mine. I enjoyed the sight of a man with a title begging for mercy. I watched tears trickle down his white chin. He promised me wealth and power, anything I wanted. With a *Pardesi* at my feet, I felt powerful again. I mocked him. Spat on his face and kicked him around. The creature just continued to beg. I made him clean the Manthrashaala with his hands and he tended to my wounds.

He cooked for me and I made him watch me eat. From time to time, I threw him some food and watched him eat it off the ground.' Kethaki smiled.

'Several days passed and the *Paradesi* suffered every insult and pain I inflicted upon him. He brought me animals and men that I sacrificed to appease my Gods. He did everything I asked him to. And I finally agreed to go to his land. Not out of pity for the *Pardesi* dog. But for vengeance. The *Jendhu* had to be destroyed and I had to take it by surprise.

I transformed myself into the *Pardesi*. Wore his attire and spoke his tongue. He stayed in a garrison by the Castle. The first day in the Castle, I buried six metallic *Rekha Yantras* around the castle. The magic in these devices would contain the beast to the castle.'

'And on the second day, I decided to appear before the beast. As I entered the room, I saw him sit on air in his triumphant posture with only one toe touching the ground. He was proud. Demons and spirits circumvented him. For a moment, I was proud of my creation. The beauty of it. And then the thought of Karshanya woke me. At first, he didn't see through the magic that disguised me. He was not powerful enough to see through it. He commanded me to kneel. And then I did. And then with every grain of rage, I pulled out the urn with the ashes as I had done before. I shouted out the name that I always addressed him with.

The name he resented- *Jendhu*.' Nathan watched as Kethaki's voice got louder.

'But this time, the beast was too fast for me. He burst into a cloud of dust and took form next to me. He pinned me to the wall and grabbed the urn from my hands to smash it against the floor. The beast had learned to control the priest. The *Jendhu* had seen through me. He gestured in the air, and my disguise disappeared. He threw me to the ground and sat on my chest laughing, poking his lamp staff up my nostrils. The beast shut his eyes and the room began to rumble and then, crashing through the door Charles's bruised body came flying.'

'He held Charles up with the tip of his claws and threw him next to me. The beast didn't want to kill us. He would have been generous if he had. Instead, he chained me to this to live forever. To watch him become a God. And Charles was to serve him for the rest of eternity. To feed him with blood and flesh. And as the ultimate punishment, the beast would rip him apart every single night only to be reborn the next day to relive the pain. Charles held on. He could run but the beast would hunt down his son. Even the strongest of men after a time, lose resolve. And when the pain became more than he could bear, Charles finally came to me begging to end it all.

I had with me the *Kriyabhasma*. Ashes from the priest's inceptive transformation ritual. My last act of mercy to a man was the *Kriyabhasma*. And one night, after sending his wife and son away from the castle, Charles went to the beast with the ashes smeared on his body. The beast ripped through his stomach and pulled apart his body limb by limb. But this time, Charles did not cry in pain and instead, he smiled. He was never going to rise again. The *Kriyabhasma* gave him his end.

The next day, the *Jendhu* was enraged. He rampaged through the castle killing everything that walked. He didn't have a *Yajamanan* anymore, I thought It had all ended. But the *Lobha,* greed of the white man was enough for the *Jendhu*. Soon, Lieutenant Pierce, was sent to Oberalp to investigate the killings. And what a man they sent! He, for wealth and power, knelt before the Jendhu. Pierce was rewarded well for the blood and flesh he brought the beast as offering. He grew in rank. The news of the God of Oberalp soon got out and several men came kneeling with hands folded. And every time, their prayers were answered. His fame grew out of the castle and the beast grew more powerful.

As time progressed, so did the ways of worship. Devotees devised

more ways of appeasing the *Jendhu*. Different ways of worshiping. What those creatures thought as worship, was entertainment for their lord. The cretins! carried altars that pierced through the flesh to please the creature. Fools, all of them. His priests went missing one after the other. They blamed the witch hunters, inquisitors and exorcists. But no one knew that they were all killed and devoured by the *Jendhu* himself. He never wanted anyone to be more powerful than himself.

My magic limited his movement to the castle and so, he created the *Dvipanta*. A rocking magical *Yantr* that helped him project himself to any place he wanted. But even that was only possible as long as the device rocked. Because from time to time, the priest surfaced from within and the projection was stalled. The *Dvipanta* demanded the sacrifice of blood as well, like everything associated with the beast. He tried to tame the priest within but didn't have total control over him. In time, the priest grew weaker, but that never meant he had totally disappeared.'

Chapter 6
Real Gods take sides.
All sides.
Afghanistan 2023

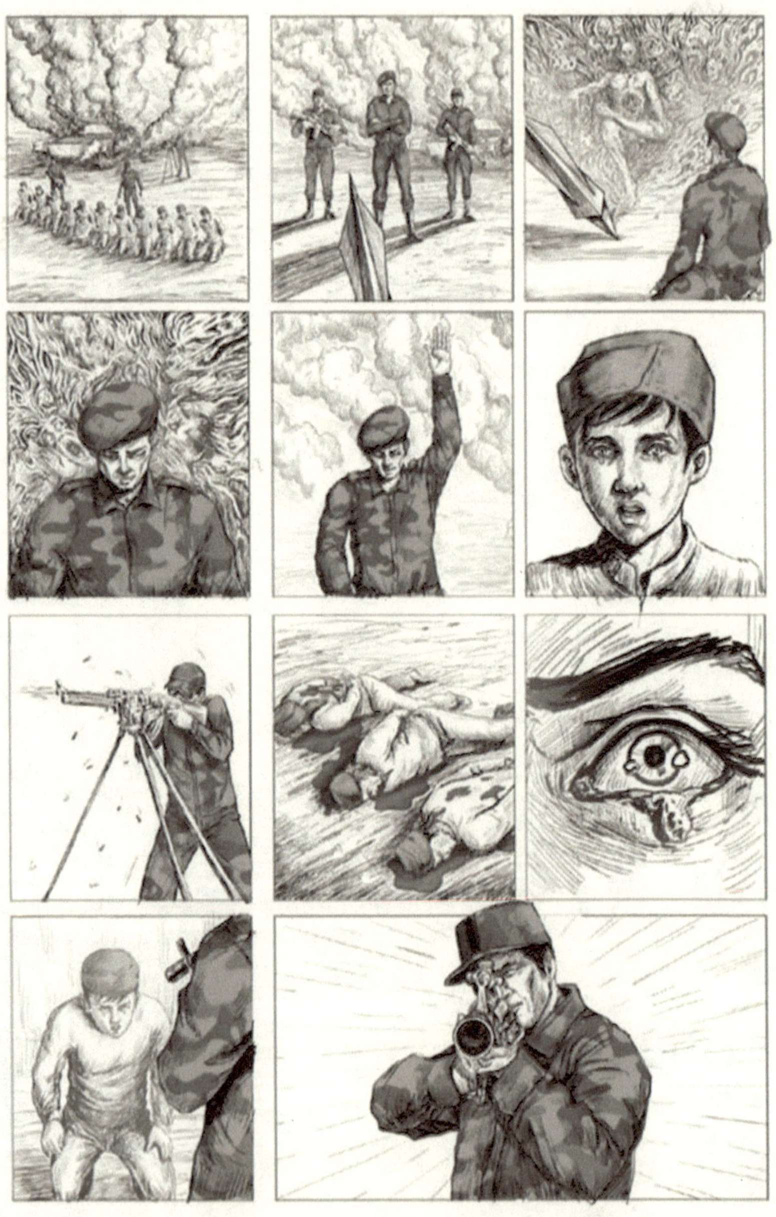

Chapter 7

Yajamanan

'You *Pardesi*, are the last of the *Yajamanan's* bloodline. And with you, the beast will complete his *Parimara*, his final transformation. He will erase the last trace of the priest from his body and that, he can do only with you on the *Yoktra*. He will then rise above every other power. Every God that man worships and every weapon that man has created.'

A few days ago, Nathan would have ignored all that he just heard. But a few days were enough to change the way he thought. Change what he believed in. He didn't know what to believe any longer. The sheer authenticity of reality, he questioned. The cloud of questions created a silent void in him.

Nathan turned around to leave. That was his first reaction. But the hallway behind him and the hall he was in had been completely transformed. Transformed beyond the sense of spatial logic. Stairs ran to the ceiling, doorways opened to the sky. Bricks lined up in haphazard patterns.

'I need to leave this place Kethaki, how do I? How did Liam get out of here? The blind painter?'

'The blind painter? Noone has ever left this place alive.'

Red dust filled the space around Nathan and Kethaki. Infernal figures formed. They smelled and licked Nathan and he began to feel them pinning him down. And ahead of him, from the dust a figure began to form. Calm and poised, with his arm resting on a large spike. With one leg folded on his lap and the toe of the other touching the ground. The demon of Oberalp. Brahma!

The infernal beings that held Nathan threw him to the demon's feet. Nathan looked up to see the demon's feet covered with the blood from the spikes from his footwear.

'The *Manthravaadhi* behind you put them in there to control me. But today, that pain fuels me.'

'That which he made to play with, plays with the world now' 'Stand *Yajamana*. Your leg I shattered; Stand on it'

Nathan heard the voice of his tormentor for the first time. It lacked a soul but it filled the air with a menacing shrill. At times, it felt like two voices, at times there was only one.

'You, *Yajamanan*, are a part of me. A part I looked over for all these years. Stronger than your father, or his father before him. Not too easy to tame. Elliot in school, got a taste of your blood didn't he? You fought back. I didn't expect that.'

'What will you have me do, beast?'

'The *Raktha Yaga* completes my *Parimara,* my transformation. That is what I have kept you alive for. The *Yajamanan* is meant to hold the reins of the *Yoktra* in the transformation. I will burn once again in the *Rudragni* killing the only traces of the wretched priest within me. And then I will be reborn as the

Rudrajeevi. A being stronger than anything else.

Stronger than any force in this cosmos. Stronger than the Gods who built it. Kethaki will bear witness to my rebirth and a new regime.'

'And I thought it only appropriate to have a couple of spectators from your side as well.'

The far side of the hall lit up and Liam appeared carrying Holly and Eva on his shoulders. Liam, the blind painter Nathan had left his children with. The only man he trusted. Nathan scurried towards them slipping with every step. But as he came closer, the space dimmed and they disappeared.

' The painter, my instrument. I gouged out his eyes so that I could see through him. His paintings that hang on your wall Yajamanan, I could see you through every one of them. I've watched your children grow. You will do anything for those children. You see their mother in them don't you? The woman you once loved. The woman whose honor you tried to protect. I was a witness to everything *Yajamanan.* You could also say that I was the manipulator of it all. You thought you were living your destiny. It was me all the time.'

A spiraling stairway formed around Nathan and he tumbled violently down the steps and came crashing on a cold floor. Nathan blacked out.

Nathan could see through the darkness of his unconscious state.

'Stand up creature.' Nathan heard. His mother's face appeared. 'Your birth brought the worst in your father.' she shouted at him and spat.

He sees his mother carry a baby into a car where his father slept drunk.

'Hide yourself son' a voice came from behind him. 'Here, hide yourself with this.' His father held out a bottle of toner ink. Nathan jumped forward and began to wipe the toner ink off his father's face to see it at least once in his life.

As he wiped off the ink, he revealed Holly's face. He picked up the child and began to run. And then, looked at her. A demon had replaced his child. He dropped it and stepped back. The demon changed back into the child. The dream rivaled reality.

'You killed our mother didn't you?' Holly shouted pointing at Nathan. 'You killed mama'. His mute child questioned him. Nathan crawled to his daughter who stepped on his fingers crushing them on the floor. He looked up to see Eva. 'You took us in, in remorse. For our mother Eva shouted.

'Stop Holly' Eva said from behind him. 'He is our papa.' Eva brought him a bowl of water. The water turned red. 'That's what's left of mama. Perhaps you would like to drink that as well'. Eva stood with her hand bleeding into the bowl. Nathan threw the bowl down and looked at her bleeding hands. The blood dripped profusely and started to fill the crevices between the blocks on the floor forming a spider web. Nathan was now tangling in the web that filled every bit of space around him. He struggled to free his arms, but red hands shot out of the web and pulled him back. Nathan shouted, but not a sound came out from within. The web formed into a long string that dangled off Brahma's nails. Brahma swung him like a pendulum. 'In time *Paradesi*…in time'.

In another room in Castle Oberalp, Eva and Holly sat huddled up on the floor. As they watched, red incantations started to form around them. And from the incantations formed beasts. Red and screaming. They started to get closer.

Eva shivered in fear but Holly, the younger one, sat composed. She continued to play with strips of paper. The red dust and the monsters it formed, got closer to the children. But in a snap, they vanished like something called them.

Eva looked around. There was nothing. She hugged her sister crying. Not out of pain or fear. But for the fact that her little sister was oblivious to everything around her.

'How can you not see all this Holly? How can you not be scared?

'It's Unni's *Achan*. Why are you scared of Unni's *Achan*?' asked Holly. Eva fainted.

Nathan lay tortured by the dreams and voices in his mind. And then he felt something rocking him gently. He strained to open his eyes. His eyelids were held shut by the dried blood that ran from the wound on his forehead. With his aching fingers, Nathan pulled his eyelids up. He could not recognize the figure that woke him up. All he could comprehend was that his voice had compassion.

'You need to wake up Nathan. Only you can end this all.'

'Kethaki, is that you?' Kethaki was the last person Nathan had seen before he blacked out. Nathan could not recognize the form in front of him. Disorientation had done that to him.

'Your curse Nathan, and your blessing are one and the same. That, what is responsible for your wounds can also heal you. That, which can bring life, can also destroy. The power to destroy the beast, the Demon that calls himself Brahma, is the *Devagni*. And the Devagni burns right here. In Oberalp.'

The strength in the speaker's voice confused Nathan even further. He had learned to question everything around him. Reality itself was questionable. Though he could not see the speaker, he thought it was Kethaki.

'How Kethaki, where?'

'The only place where he cannot venture. Around the castle are four devices that barricade him to these walls. The watchtower to the south of the castle holds the *Eternal Devaagni*. Burning for hundreds of years. The Devagni and the Rudragni are the eternal flames that maintain cosmic balance. Brahma is a child of the Rudrani. Get to the Devagni and you will find a way to destroy the demon.'

And saying that, the faint figure disappeared. Not waiting to answer any more questions or to whisper any more secrets.

Nathan sat up and thought for a while. He had to get logical. He had to pull himself together.

The lives of his children also depended on what Nathan did.

The space around him started to make sense. He realised that he was housed inside a cellar in the castle. At the entrance to the cellar, infernal beings formed of red dust, kept guard. They howled and screamed. Breaking apart and forming again. Changing faces and forms. Nathan could not get past these things. He could not overpower that which did not exist. But as he stood up, the creatures disappeared. Nathan was now free to exit the cellar.

Outside the cellar, Nathan made his way through the long passage. All he had to do was head south and look for a tower. Nathan lost his way around Oberalp, but the voice that had woken him, guided him through. A part of him did not want to trust the voice. Was it Kethaki? He asked himself. But there was something in the voice that Nathan gave him some hope. Soon Nathan stood facing the South Tower. That itself, was a monster. At some time, the tower watched over the wealth of Oberalp. Today, it housed within it a secret that could free Nathan and his children from a curse. The door into the tower had not been opened in ages. And it was heavy. Nathan struggled to move the heavy door and the rusted hinges growled . Inside the tower, a long tiring spiral staircase took Nathan to the guard's room. Nathan struggled up the steps, dragging his bad leg.

The glow of the Devagni lit the walls of the stairwell. The sight was breathtaking. Nathan had seen nothing like it. The Devagni burnt high up in the air above a stone altar. It did not charr the wood that fueled it. Four golden rings circumvented the Devagni. Nathan stretched his hand out to touch the eternal flame. It did not feel warm. It did not burn. The rings moved around and encased the flame to form a glowing globular mass. Nathan could not feel the weight in his hand. It just sat there levitating above his palm. For a moment, Nathan felt a sanctity he had never felt before. He was in the presence of a force very pure. He pulled his hand back slowly. The flame moved along. With care, he carried the flame down the tower. The flame flickered changing colors from blue to orange to yellow mesmerizing the eyes that looked into it.

Nathan had the flame but he didn't quite know what to do with it. Probably Kethaki knew. The passages of Oberalp were not guarded anymore. Nathan walked on puzzled. Probably the beast saw everything. Maybe he didn't. Nathan didn't want to think too deep into that. He didn't know the voice that helped him navigate through the passages of Oberalp. But he knew it was one that didn't want to hurt him.

Kethaki strained his eyes to look towards the footsteps that approached him. With his head tied back with his hair, any movement meant excruciating pain. The glow from the Devagni filled the room. Light hurt Kethaki's eyes. It was not something he was used to.

'*Pardesi*, the *Devagni* how do you have it? I thought you were locked away. How did you get out?'

Kethaki never expected to see Nathan again.

'You! You told me how to get it. I thought you came into my cell and told me that it was hidden in the South Tower.'

'How do you think I can set myself free? And the *Devagni* is something I have no knowledge of. The *Devanaars* are the keepers of the flame. It is only they who know how to invoke the *Devagni*. The flame that glows without burning the wood in the altar that prepares it. That is not a craft that I am aware of. And the last person who knew it was Devabrahma Devanaar. The priest who has become the demon that torments us.'

Loud whirring sounds echoed through the walls of the castle rattling the stone walls and pillars. The sound shot through Nathan's ears and he sat holding his head. He felt like his skull would be crushed. The *Devagni* that was in his hands levitated on thin air but the sound made it flicker violently. The inherent calmness of the flame was lost. The sound did that. The menacing whirling sound.

Nathan followed to sound till he could feel the vibrations against his chest. He looked down into the large courtyard. A ritual had taken form. Oberalp that was empty moments ago was filled with people. They had markings of Brahma's fangs.

Their bodies adorned with incantations. They looked like people, but didn't feel human. In the center of the courtyard was a large step well and on each of the steps, men sat prostrating before Brahma who sat on thin air. They all looked like followers. Followers of a God who gave them everything they wanted without consideration of cosmic balance. A demon who had grown into a God.

Men swung large metal sounders on a red chain. These things produced the loud whirling sound. The sound that ripped across Nathan's body. The spikes on the sounders cut the men, but that didn't stop them. The blood was their offering to their Lord. Other men spun around in a trance carrying large demonic altars. The spikes on them driving through the bearer's flesh. Blood shot across the floor. Every act of worship demanded this blood. Brahma sat pleased.

'The *Raktha Yaga* has commenced *Pardesi*. It's time to be summoned by the *Jendhu*. This is the day he has been waiting for. This is the day he has kept you alive for. Every day of your life that he tormented you and broke you, was in preparation for this.'

Kethaki struggled to shout out to Nathan. Nathan could not move. Transfixed by the sight of the ritual. Shocked to see the bloody spectacle that unraveled in front of him. He feared what he saw. He feared what would come.

'Yajamanasya Swagathamasthi'.

Nathan hears the words rumble like thunder. 'Witness the spectacle that will birth the future God of this cosmos.' Red dust danced in the air and figures of demons formed in them. The demons formed a cage and inside that, floated Holly and Eva. They floated without motion. The eyes look around in fear.

Nathan ran back to Kethaki.

'You have to help me save my children Kethaki. You are the only one who can.'

Nathan had lived a life of peril but this was worse than his most terrible nightmares. This was something he couldn't wake up from.

'Look at me *Pardesi*! I have been rotting for hundreds of years. I'm a soul caged inside a dead body. The *Jendhu* today is more powerful than I could have made him. You ask me for help. There was a time when I could control the beast with the ashes of his wife and son. But with the priest inside him dying with every day, that is not possible anymore. During the *Rakhtha Yaaga*, the *Jendhu* must make himself vulnerable. And that happens only at the *Yoktra*. And then he will burn in the *Rudragni*. In its purest form, without the *Devagni* to balance, it can make a being both strong and malevolent.'

Nathan's lips shivered out of helplessness.

'The demon needs to burn in the *Devagni*. Do not let him complete the Yaaga.' A voice came from behind Nathan. A silhouetted figure appeared at a distance from Nathan and Kethaki. Nathan could not see the face of the man who spoke to him. But he recognised the voice. It was the voice that spoke to him in the cellar and guided him to the South Tower. And then the silhouette disappeared before Nathan could run to him.

Nathan reached for the *Devagni*. It rested above his palm. He ran out and down the stairs that lead to the atrium. Brahma's votaries began to run to him shouting in a menacing tongue. They pinned Nathan to the ground. Nathan lost grip of the *Devagni* and it floated away from the crowd. Nathan could not move. The men picked him up and hit him. Nathan recognized the faces of a few of his attackers. These are men he had seen. Powerful men. Mob kings, politicians, men of power. Today he knew where the power came from. They dragged him down the step well and made him kneel. Brahma descended and floated above a structure made of red rope and wood. The ropes from the contraption ran all the way to where Nathan sat. Nathan felt his palms burn. He lifted his hands and saw that two golden gauntlets with incantations had formed around his palm and fingers. The metal burnt his skin. He tried to remove it, but then it burned hotter.

'The *Hasthapa, Yajamanan* around your hands will let you control the

Yoktra. It was made for Karshanya. The boy could never use it. He was not strong enough. It's time to take your seat *Yajamanan.* Steer me through the Median and light the *Rudragni.*'

'To the *Fiends of the Median,* I will sacrifice these lowlifes who bleed for me. And at the end of it all, comes the final sacrifice. The sacrifice of the *Yajamanan* to free the *Rudrajeevi* from the harness of the *Yoktra.* You, *Yajamana,* will set fire to me with the *Rudraagni.* Today, we cremate the priest. Today, Brahma will be free of Brahmadeva Devanaar. The one that contaminates me.'

As Brahma spoke, a large cauldron filled with water appeared and above it an aggressive vigorous flame. The *Rudragni.* That which gave creatures virility and strength. The flame that mixed with the *Devagni* to form man. The ropes from the *Yoktra* rose and knotted around the gauntlets on Nathans hands. Nathan was not in control of his body anymore. Long red shrouds came floating in and orbited the *Rudraagni.*

Nathan knew he was not powerful enough for the abomination he confronted. He looked up into the cage formed by the red dust and saw the faces of his children. He did not have the strength, but he knew the one thing that could give him the strength to fight the abomination. Nathan grabbed the feet of the men who held him and pulled. They came crashing to the ground. He got up and reached out for the shrouds. Grabbing one of them, he set it on fire. Nathan had caught the beast by surprise. Brahma had failed to see Nathan's resolve.

Helplessness can make men do powerful things. Things they never thought they could do. Nathan rolled on the ground draping the red shrouds around himself till he could feel the *Rudragni* incinerate his body. Nathan screamed as his body burned. Brahma lifted his fingers and the burning body rose, but he could not put the fire out. The Rudragni shot flares in all directions scorching as hot as the sun. Nathan screamed as it consumed him. The Rudragni felt like a thousand pins pierce into Nathan's flesh. Every iota of him palpitated vigorously. He could feel his bone split away from himself and join back. But it was not only the body that felt it. In his mind, he pictured every single moment of his life and felt every pain ten folds stronger than it initially did. And at the end of it, Nathan's body flopped unconscious. The body was intact, but smoke rose from it as it glowed with a red aura.

Nathan could feel the heat, but it hadn't killed him. With his eyes shut, he could see everything around him. Or rather sense the presence of another world. Everything around Nathan turned red. So red that it hurt his eyes. But he could not shut his mind's eye. It did not have eyelids. And then, the space around him turned black. Black as the darkest night. Colder than the coldest winter in his life. Nathan lifted his head slowly. He was surrounded by people from his life. In the darkness, he saw each one of them. The kids who bullied him in school. Officers and politicians who made his life a living hell on the force. The perverted police chief Devin Absil, he had assaulted in court. The women who left him, The nefarious Theo Lauder.

'Poke him with a stick, will you? See if the cripple is dead' said one of them.

'Perhaps this will wake him up' Absil unzipped his pants and prepared to urinate on him.

Nathan sprang up and pulled up Absil's zipper. The man screamed in pain and fell back crying. He then punched the face of the woman behind him. Grabbing a can of paint, Nathan sprayed across the eyes of the boys from school. He was full of rage and energy. He ripped apart the people around him. And then, everything disappeared breaking the illusion that Nathan was in. The *Rudragni* had changed him. He was back at the *Yaaga*.

Brahma moved his fingers and the reigns of the *Yoktra* wound around Nathan again. Nathan pulled the ropes and bit on them ripping them into shreds. He went on a frenzy stabbing and slaughtering the men around him with his bare hands. He smashed their heads and broke their necks. The *Rudragni* gave him immense strength. He was no match for the men around him.

'Wield to me *Yajamanan*. Fulfill your life's destiny. The lives of your children hang by my fingers.' Brahma roared.

'Children! To hell with them! They are not even mine. All I want is to destroy you beast.' The newfound strength had a price. The *Rudragni* had killed Nathan's emotions.

The children, hearing this, began to cry. In all the years with Nathan, he had never hurt them. Holly, never even knew that he was her foster father.

'Papa why? Why do you say that?' Cried Eva.

'Shut up! This creature and I have scores to settle. Nathan scorned.

Brahma burst into red dust and took form in front of Nathan. He drove his staff up Nathan's chin and lifted him up.

'I've taken years to be to become what I am today. And you think you can do that in a day. *Yajamana?*'

Nathan set both his feet on the demon's shoulder and gained a foothold. Pushing away from the staff he reached for Brahma's face and dug his nails between the jaws. And with one uninhibited motion, pulled out the golden fangs. Brahma screamed in pain and hurled Nathan to the ground. Nathan banged the floor with his clenched fist. He caught sight of Brahma's *Methiadi* with the golden spikes. With the pointed end of the staff, Nathan pried out the spikes. Brahma kicked him. But Nathan did not stop.

The cage that held the children vanished and they fell to the ground. Eva turned around to check if her sister was alright.

She was shocked to see Holly get up and walk calmly between Brahma's votaries. Not bothered by the blood that covered the floor or the bodies on them.

The ropes of the *Yoktra* rose again and wound around Nathan's neck but he cut them with the staff. He lifted the staff and drove it through Brahma's hand and into the ground. Stepping on the fingers, he pulled out the long golden nails. With his free hand, Brahma pushed Nathan off him. He growled in anger.

The red storm began to form around him and from it rose the demons. They entered Nathan's body from all around and tossed him around like a leaf caught in the wind. Nathan convulsed intensely and fell. The fall broke his trance. He came to his senses and pushed his shoulder up with his arms. He looked around and understood the damage he had done. Nathan looked at Brahma and saw the fury within. The beast roared with pain and anger.

'*Yajamana*, you think it's the metal that makes me? My strength does not come from weapons but from the magic I have mastered. You shall complete what you started.'

Brahma rose to the *Yoktra*. The ropes flew around encircling his body. The other ends darted to Nathan and pulled him to the *Yoktra*. The *Hasthapa* formed around his hands and the ropes strung through it. Nathan's hands began to make symbols by themselves like he was not in control. He formed

figures out the ropes looped around the fingers. Brahma closed his eyes and incantations began to fill the air around the *Yoktra*. The demons in the dust howled and flew through the ropes of the Yoktra. Brahma began to grow in size. The blood oozing out of his face stopped and the crevices healed.

Nathan could feel his life being sucked out. He could not break free. He was no longer in control. The *Hasthapa* was doing all the work. It was made that way. All it needed to work was the *Yajamanan's* blood. The atrium took on a red hue. The *Yaaga* had set loose the creatures of the median and they flew around with menacing screeches. Brahma rose. It was time for him to be fired in the *Rudragni*. The earth shook and the tremors swept through the walls of Oberalp. The end of the yaaga was near.

'Unnidey Achha, look I finally learnt how to make these'. A feeble innocent voice spoke from below. Holly stood in front of the demon holding up a little paper bird.

The beast arched his head down to look at Holly. She smiled at him. Not fearing his form or the destruction he could cause.

Brahma froze.

Nathan pulled the child away and shielded her.

Brahma floated in the air. He did not move. The child's voice had done something to him. He began to shake violently. A pale image split away

from the beastly form. It had a gentle face.

'It is you! How?' the beast whispered softly.

Nathan had heard this voice before. This was the voice that spoke to him in the cellar. This was the voice that guided him to the *Devagni*. It was him all along. The innocent priest who was dying inside the demon.

The priest lifted his hands and the *Devagni* that had distanced itself from the commotion floated into the step well.

Brahma shook violently shifting between forms. 'Wretched priest' shouted the beast 'You still pollute me?'

The priest transformed back into the demon. The demon began to battle himself, changing forms. Nathan tried to remember what Kethaki had told him.

He found the shroud and tied the end to the staff. And taking aim, hurled it at the beast's heart. The staff pierced through. The beast tried to pull it out, but Nathan grabbed the shroud and sprinted around the well wrapping the demon. The Devagni had positioned itself in front of Brahma. The last length of the shroud touched the flame and caught fire. The Devagni climbed through the cloth encasing Brahma.

The beast began to burn in the inferno. Brahma tried to free himself from the shroud. But something had weakened him. The creature drove his fingers into his own chest and ripped it. The fire caught on. Nathan grabbed Holly and ran to Eva. The worshippers had come out of their trance, and many ran out of the atrium. Some watched the spectacle transfixed. Nathan took the children in his arms. As they looked towards the entrance, the souls from the Field of Wanderers walked into the atrium to the step well.

'We bear witness' They said in unison and walked into the fire. They were now free.

The *Devagni* raged devouring and setting everything free. It changed in color and when it had consumed everything, it calmed down. The flame took on a cool blue aura.

Nathan saw a form emerging from the flame. At first, the form was hazy but then, it looked human.

Brahmadeva, in priestly attire, walked out. He glowed intensely. He walked to Nathan and the children looking around the atrium.

'Vengeance had created a demon out of me. I let it consume me and by the time I saw the destruction it could cause, It was too powerful. The Devagni you found Nathan, I had lit years before. It waited for the right hands. You, Nathan were not only destined to free the Demon off me, but to also free the world from his hands. The demon possessed many in your life. Your mother, the men who harmed you and every obstacle you faced. As he manipulated them to break you, I tried, like a dying candle, to shed some light into your life'.

Devabrahma sat and touched Holly on the cheeks.

'Unnidey Achaa' said Holly. Nathan and Holly did not understand the language.

'Daathi Kutty !' A final tear rolled down the priest's eye and he vanished.

Holly fell into Nathan's arms unconscious. Eva shook her and slowly, she opened her eyes.

'Who was that paapa?' she asks trying to make sense of everything around her.

'I don't know who you became or the words you spoke Eva. But you were more powerful than all the evil in the world combined.'

Nathan hugged his children. He got up and walked out of Oberalp hoping to never look back or even dream of the place. The trees that engulfed the castle retracted to the ground and the incantations faded off the walls. Castle Oberalp now showed signs only of its age, not of the master that reigned in it.

But not everything had changed. Curses have a way of standing through time. In the darkness within the castle, dripping with blood and rotting, entangled in the web sewn by the *Jendhu*, lived on Kethaki to bear witness, of times to come.

Chapter 8
Generations

A few years later...

Greens and blues sputtered out of the nozzle onto the wall. The hand that held the cans gently glided over the mural. Crowds looked on as a bright eighteen-year-old gave the finishing touches to a towering 30-foot mural. It depicted children erecting an uprooted tree. Bright in color, the mural made everyone smile. The painter took a few moments to look up at her accomplishment. She then turned to face the reporters, wiping her forehead with an old rag.

'As an artivist, what is it that you are trying to say through this painting.'
The young girl smiled.
'We are a generation that has inherited the outcomes of greed and deception. The world we inherited is broken and we are left to mend it. My mural depicts not the raising of a flag in celebration of the victory of a mindless war. But the values that today's generation upholds. A tree links our past, present and future. The seed planted by our fathers, we water and nurse it. The fruits are for our children.'
From a short distance, Natan and Eva watched along with the crowd.
Holly, born without a voice, now spoke louder than anyone.

Addendum

1. Thirumeni: A respectful way of addressing a person. Usually a priest.
2. Swami Daasa Bhavathi. Daasarshy Swami Bhavathi: The master will become the slave and the slave, the master.
3. Yoktra: Harness
4. Nigrah: Stop!
5. Deva: A male deity
6. Naaduvaazi: Chieftain of a province.
7. Sarvagyani: One who knows everything
8. Umbra: A colloquial form of *Thamburan*. Landlords and men of power were addressed as *Thamburan* by people from the lower strata of society.
9. Viswakarma: The architect of the Gods and the Patron deity of craftsmen
10. Neiappam: A sweet fried snack prepared with jaggery and rice dough.
11. Amma: Mother
12. Achha/Achhan: Father
13. Thiruviza: Festival
14. Manthravaadi: Magician
15. Illam: House
16. Manthrashaala: A place where a Magician/Occultist or occultist performs his rituals
17. Yajamanan: Guardian of a spirit in the context of the story. The Yajamanan is responsible to keep the spirit happy.
18. Yajamanasya Swagathamasthi: Welcome, Yajamanan
19. Pavakooth: A traditional puppet show.
20. Yaagam: An elaborate sacrificial ritual performed to appease the Gods. A Yaagam is performed by a priest in front of a fire into which several sacrificial offerings are placed.

21. Devapreethi: Appeasing the Gods.
22. Maha: Large
23. Yaaga Aacharyan: A priest who heads a Yaagam.
24. Dwarapalak: Gatekeeper
25. Vaithari: A verse, mostly lyrical, made up to memorise something.
26. Valayam: Circle
27. Hasthapa: Metal gauntlet
28. Methiadi: The wooden footwear usually worn by priests
29. Jendhu: Animal. Derogatory in the context of the story.
30. Nilavara: A room used to store things in a traditional house.
31. Kutty: Child
32. Pardesi: Foreigner
33. Yantr: Device
34. Lobha: Greed
35. Parimara: Transformation
36. Baishka: Sort of a rage-filled cry in the line of 'meat of a hunted animal'.
37. Aham Jighasmu: I am destruction

www.ingramcontent.com/pod-product-compliance
Lightning Source LLC
LaVergne TN
LVHW090219180726
843492LV00012B/2025